As I remember it

This is an IndieMosh book

brought to you by MoshPit Publishing
an imprint of Mosher's Business Support Pty Ltd

PO Box 4363
Penrith NSW 2750

indiemosh.com.au

Copyright © Jenny Kroonstuiver 2021

The moral right of the author has been asserted in accordance with the Copyright Amendment (Moral Rights) Act 2000.

All rights reserved. Except as permitted under the Australian Copyright Act 1968 (for example, fair dealing for the purposes of study, research, criticism or review) no part of this publication may be reproduced, stored in a retrieval system, or transmitted in any form or by any means, electronic, mechanical, photocopying, recording or otherwise, without the written permission of the publisher.

 A catalogue record for this work is available from the National Library of Australia

https://www.nla.gov.au/collections

Title:	As I remember it
Subtitle:	The Lina Graebner diaries
Author:	Lina Graebner
Compiler:	Kroonstuiver, Jenny
ISBNs:	9781922703453 (paperback)
	9781922703460 (ebook – epub)
	9781922703477 (ebook – Kindle)
Subjects:	**BIOGRAPHY & AUTOBIOGRAPHY**/Personal Memoirs; Historical; Women; Survival

This book is memoir. It reflects the author's recollections of experiences over time. Any editing has been merely to improve the experience for the reader. As such, the editor/compiler and publisher can take no responsibility for the content herein.

Cover concept by Jenny Kroonstuiver

Photo collection supplied by the Graebner family

Cover design and layout by Sarah Davies www.instagram.com/lemon.design.studios

As I remember it

The Lina Graebner diaries

Compiled by Jenny Kroonstuiver

This book is dedicated to Lina's father, mother, sisters and brothers in-law, as well as all those who, at great personal risk, provided support and assistance contributing to her family's survival during their escape from persecution and oppression by Joseph Stalin's leadership of the Soviet Union and then their journey through Europe during the second World War.

Снявши го́лову, по волоса́м не пла́чут
"After taking off the head, one shouldn't grieve over the hair".

Russian proverb

Contents

Introduction 1

Chapter 1 – Siberian heritage 4

Chapter 2 – 1937, Crimea 16

Chapter 3 – 1941, Caucasus 38

Chapter 4 – 1943, leaving Russia 62

Chapter 5 – Yugoslavia 76

Chapter 6 – 1945, Austria 87

Chapter 7 – Refugee camps in Austria 100

Chapter 8 – Arrival in Australia 116

Chapter 9 – Marriage 131

Chapter 10 – Children 145

Chapter 11 – After Kalgoorlie 163

Epilogue 177

Acknowledgements 180

About Jenny Kroonstuiver 182

As I remember it

Introduction

My name is Galina Petrovna (daughter of Peter) Gerzen. I was born in 1931 in Siberia, in a town called Irtyshsk on the river Irtysh – now part of modern-day Kazakhstan. My mother was born in Omsk. My grandparents migrated to Siberia from the Volga region. My parents were the first 'free born' Siberians at the beginning of the 20th century. They loved their homeland, Siberia, a very different story from the people who were later sentenced to Siberia, where few survived their sentences. My Siberian roots are of free settlers.

In 1935 my parents moved to Crimea in the hope of escaping the terror of communism. I remember clearly standing by the train window spellbound by the scenery of the Ural Mountains in particular. Father was a high-school teacher and qualified in two languages, German and Russian.

From 1935 until autumn 1937, we lived in a semi-rural town, big enough to accommodate a full secondary education system.

In 1938, on arrival of my mother's sister and her family from Siberia, we moved to another town. We lived there until the commencement of World War II in 1941.

Having been classified as German Russians, we were moved to Caucasus in that year, where we lived for one year and three months in an unoccupied village and experienced not only the fighting front but also a mouse plague. There we also buried our little brother on a hill top. He could not chew wheat and that was all we had to eat, so he died of starvation.

In 1942 we returned to Crimea to relative peace, away from the fighting front and the mouse plague.

The Lina Graebner Diaries

In 1943 we began our exodus from Russia to Germany. After crossing the Black Sea from Yevpatoriya to Odessa we were taken to Poland to be 'cleaned' and 'deloused'. We were then moved to a camp in Austria. Towards the end of 1943 we went to Yugoslavia as part of a work force on a farm. We spent a full year there.

In 1945, with the approach of the Russians, we headed for Austria and the British sector on foot, as did thousands of others, running from the Russians and their reputation for unspeakable atrocities.

We arrived in Klagenfurt, Austria, in the summer of 1945 where we were joined by thousands of people fleeing from the Eastern Bloc countries, all those countries which had been occupied and terrorised by the Russians. It seemed that all of humanity was on the run from evil, the evil of Russian communism.

We lived in the bombed-out buildings of Klagenfurt fed by the soup kitchens, a 'ladle-full-of-something' a day. The world could not ignore the many thousands of people that eventually grew into millions. Camps were erected in most cities in Austria, three thousand per camp, 50 per army barracks. This refugee camp pattern was also followed in Germany. Eventually all refugees were placed in camps.

In 1950, Australia volunteered to take some refugees and we were among that number. We arrived in Fremantle, Western Australia, in September 1950. Our first stay was in the Northam army camp until we were all placed in a work situation. This was not too difficult as we were all under a two-year contract to work where we were placed.

In early 1951 the Water Supply Board built a Nissen hut camp in Kelmscott in the bush, a couple of miles from the Albany Highway. My family lived there for close to two years.

In December 1953, I married an Australian, Andrew Graebner, and together we built our Australian family and life.

As I remember it

The Gerzen family, 1935

Chapter 1 – Siberian heritage

My mother's mother, my grandmother, came from quite an elite family. My father from a humble one.

My grandmother married 'beneath' herself, as the term was used at that time. However, she and my grandfather were extremely happy as a couple, proving wrong all who said they were mismatched. My grandmother was a 'lady' in every sense. Grandfather was a working-class man who laboured his way up to a managerial position in a large factory making bricks, dealing with a lot of machinery.

My grandmother ran the household and a lot more that came her way. They were both Christians, with a strong faith. The church meant a lot to them and took a lot of their time and resources, but they did it with love as they loved their church. As they prospered, their responsibility towards others increased. They were very generous and a stream of people in need came and went.

I am speaking of a time around 10 years into the 20th century. People were very dependent on each other for the basics, sometimes even for survival itself. My grandparents were Volga Germans who had emigrated to Siberia with a very young family. My mother, and later her sister Lydia, were both born in Siberia. For my grandparents it was a chance to own more land, with opportunities to do well for those who were intelligent, worked hard and generally applied themselves to a very different way of life. My grandparents scored well on all fronts and prospered.

Their way of life was very different, dictated by the climate, where the choices are to apply oneself or perish. In Siberia, there are only three months in which to grow, harvest and store. For six months everything is covered in snow. Then there are six weeks of spring and thawing, and a further six weeks of autumn, with early flurries of snow which stayed put for six months. During this time, all activity had to take place indoors. Even all the animals had to be indoors.

My mother was born in 1906 in Omsk, which used to be the capital city of Siberia. She remembered her father being away fighting a war (possibly the Russo-Japanese war). He was away for something like five years and when he came back, he was like a stranger. Five years is a long time out of a child's life. What's more, he was not well, as he contracted malaria which cost him his life when he was only around 60 years old.

At least Mum had a father into adulthood. In fact, she was already married when he died. My mother not only took care of her mother, but also of her younger sister who was 10 years younger than she.

I like this part of my mother's life because it is so romantic. Mother did not get a tertiary education – she went into apprenticeship to train as a dressmaker. Her mother always felt bad about it, and she used to say, "Paulina, you deserve better. You are bright."

Her father said, "This is your aristocratic background talking. There is nothing wrong with having a useful skill and the rest is up to her. She is literate."

He had a point, and Mum proved him right. She educated herself; she read and read and read. At 18 she met her future husband, who was a medical student. They courted and married before she was 20. She completed her training and became a highly skilled dressmaker. She felt a little self-conscious about not having a higher education, but need not have worried as she could hold her own with any of her husband's intellectual friends.

It was a little embarrassing at times when, thinking she was a teacher, people would say, "Why does your wife not work in her profession?"

Mother would say: "I *am* working in my field. I am a dressmaker."

Her husband was very proud of her. He would often say, "Good on you for putting them in their place."

She would reply: "But darling, that is what I am."

He would encourage her by saying, "You are more of an intellectual than any of them. You just don't have a little piece of paper to present to the world and say, 'Look, I am qualified'."

They were extremely happy. Mother gave birth to a girl, Lucya, in 1926, and they all felt life just could not be better. Mother insisted on her younger sister, Lydia, qualifying in something, and she sent her to university to get a degree in accounting. That was unusual for a female at the beginning of the 20th century.

I know so little about my grandparents. I was only three when my grandmother died, and my memories of her are from stories my mother told me. My grandfather died before I was born, but everything I heard about them made me realise what very special people they were. My mother was good testimony to the kind of people who gave her this foundation, which no amount of evil could ever destroy. In fact, the experience of evil that touched her so many times in years to come, made her stronger.

A forced *Galadovka*, starvation, nearly cost all of them their lives. Miraculously, they survived when nearly the whole town died, except for the law enforcers, of course. The reason for their survival was that the town was short of doctors, and my mother's husband was a doctor. My mother and her husband received survival rations, but nothing for her mother or her sister, it was just for Mum, her husband

and their child, Lucya. The rations had to be stretched to two more adults. How they made it was a miracle. Many poor starving people made their way to the doctor's surgery for help, and some froze in their tracks and remained there. My mother said that, after a while, there were so many people near their place that they were afraid to go near the window so as not to see the frozen corpses. In the end, they seemed to be moving to the centre of any given room, mother said. When spring came, there was another danger, of infections and disease, as there were no people left to bury the dead.

Three years after my mother was married, her husband died in the line of duty. He had saved a patient and paid with his life. His last words were, "I don't want to die, I don't want to die. Where is my daughter?" At night her cot was on his side of the bed, and when she called, he stretched out his arm and held her with his hands until she fell asleep. My mother was devastated at his death. He was only 26 years old, and she was a widow at 22. Her mother was a tower of strength to her as she worried that she might lose a daughter as well, my mother was so terribly affected. There was nothing anyone could do to comfort her. She was inconsolable.

One of the things her mother used to say to her over and over again was, "Paulina, if you lay next to Peter and got buried with him it would not make the slightest difference to him. This is the finality of death. He is no longer here, and you cannot follow him. Look at your daughter, she is alive, she cannot do without you, without your love. Focus on that."

She had a lot of support from a lot of people, but the waste of it all, a young, beautiful person dying, just did not make sense. He had survived a *Galadovka* only to die while saving another. This amounted to a whole lot of contradiction in my mother's eyes.

My mother and her husband had belonged to the local repertory. They both loved the theatre. The long winters with very short days created an ideal environment for cultural pursuits and the theatre was one of them: the other was literature. As all work had to be done indoors, in a confined space, they would choose a fluent reader to while the rest of the people worked. Mother said they read *War And Peace* from cover to cover more than once, as well as the French classics. They read them all. On the lighter side they knew Scottish poet and lyricist Robert 'Rabbie' Burns as if he was theirs. They were familiar with Shakespeare and the British classics. Charles Dickens was another other well-known to them.

It was in the circle of theatre and literature that she met my father, her second husband. In fact, before her first husband's death, he was one of their special friends. There was one obstacle to their friendship, though: Father said he fell in love with her the moment he laid eyes on her, when she was a happily married woman. He felt guilty about it and therefore stayed out of their way whenever he could. It really bothered him. His family belonged to the strict reformed church. I doubt he would have been able to marry Mum, who belonged to another church, but the revolution changed all that. Bibles were burnt and priests shot and, in return, the people received atheism, but it was his religious foundation that made Father feel strongly that you marry for life and, as Mum was already married, end of story. He avoided being alone with her or portraying a role in a play opposite her, as he just could not bear it.

My father was just as shocked at the death of such a gifted young doctor as the rest of the community. All seemed to be grieving for this special person, their doctor. Again, Father felt guilty at the thought that he might have a chance of having his love returned now that Mother was no longer married. The fact that she had a child, a mother to support and a sister, was all irrelevant. He loved her with all his heart, as only a 20-year-old can, without any reservations. He would see her at gatherings, watch her hurting and grieving, going outside to weep and returning with a stained face. He said it nearly killed him to see her suffer like that, with him being helpless to comfort her.

After a few months, he was tempted to go to her and declare his love, but when he faced her and saw the pain etched into her face, he kept silent and waited. The opportunity presented itself when Father was transferred to a new teaching post, which meant he would be away for the whole teaching year. He could not go away without telling her of his feelings. It was only six months after Mum's husband's death, too soon to be free to love again, yet, she was faced with a decision.

He told her of how much he loved her and that he was not insensitive to her grief, but he could not leave without telling her of his feelings and at least ask her to wait for him. Mother was very perplexed. No, she was not ready to love and commit herself wholly and anything less would not be fair to him.

Once again, she sought her mother's advice, whose answer was simple, "Nothing in the world will bring Peter back. You have to think of the living, not the dead. The dead don't need you, the living cannot live without your love. Think about it. If you let him go for a year, he is not going to live in isolation, he is going to move on. A lot of his colleagues will be young, beautiful females, so do you want to take that kind of risk?"

Mother was very touched by this beautiful man, his honourable intentions and his overwhelming love for her. She accepted his proposal. They married and went together to his new post. His name was also Peter, Peter Gerzen, which was a nice coincidence. Her daughter Lucya, now two-and-a-half years old, referred to him as 'the handsome uncle'. The transition seemed pain-free for Lucya as she was so little and had few recollections of her own father.

There was only one rather big sadness. Mum's mother-in-law resented the marriage bitterly. For her, it was too soon after her son's death and she could not forgive Mum and severed all contact, which included her granddaughter. On one occasion Mother was in Omsk with Lucya when she saw her mother-in-law coming towards her. She kneeled at Lucya's feet, hugged her passionately and wept, without identifying herself to the little one who was about five at the time. It was very, very sad. Mother just watched helplessly as the grandmother hugged her granddaughter.

To Mother she just said, "You have betrayed him," and disappeared into the crowd. Mother was shocked. More than two years had passed since her husband died, and yet, his mother had not healed or softened towards her. Lucya asked her mother why this lady was hugging her and crying. Mother said it was probably because she had lost a little one her size. What else could she say? She told me this story often, so it could not have been too comfortable for her to keep reflecting on that experience.

Twelve months after mother married my father, she gave birth to her first child with her new husband in 1930, a little girl, Irma. They were very happy.

For Lucya, Dad's transformation from handsome uncle to 'Daddy' just happened. Only once did she recall her own father, but it quickly disappeared into the mists of time. It occurred because of a lamp my mother and her first husband had bought together in company with Lucya, a beautiful table lamp that still stood on my father's writing desk. Lucya once spilled some water on the desk, which damaged some of his writing material kept under glass. He took her by the hand and explained that everything on this table was his work. She had no reason to ever play on it or touch anything on that table. Did she understand? She just nodded. Mum went outside and wept: she was with child, which made her more vulnerable. After Dad had left for school, Lucya came up for comfort and they both settled down. It was then that Lucya said, "Mummy, Dad said that everything on his desk was his, but it isn't. We bought the lamp."

Mum then asked, "Who bought the lamp?" Lucya replied, "You and I and Daddy."

When Mum asked where Daddy was now, Lucya thought for a while before finally replying, "At school". Mother was sad at not being able to keep Lucya's father's memory alive, but she was certain that her seeing my father and the rest of the family as hers, as one, was very important.

Father put himself out far more for Lucya than for his own two children, my sister and me. He knew he was walking a tightrope regarding his freedom, and it seemed he knew he would not see any of us as adults. He never wanted Lucya to look back after losing him and say, "This is why he gave more love to the other two."

Mother gave birth to three children with my father; but one died soon after birth. My parents were extremely happy. Maybe the cloud of uncertainty made them appreciate each moment of their nine years together. As a teacher, father went from strength to strength. He did a lot of post-graduate studies and was qualified as a teacher in two languages, German and Russian. He was very much in demand as a 'pedagogue'. This is the commonly used term in Russia for 'teacher'. Teachers are held in the highest esteem. Only scientists came ahead of teachers, followed by engineers, doctors and dentists, who were at the bottom of the scale of status in Russia. Life was dispensable, and not many resources were channelled in the direction of health or welfare of the people.

In her early 30s Mother once again went through a *Galadovka*[1] starvation. I was 18 months old at the time and still breastfeeding. I would never have made it otherwise. My grandmother was still living with Mum, as was her sister. Once again, the rations given were only for Father's family and yet had to stretch to two more adults. Again, people froze in the streets. One day, Father came home with a greatly reduced ration. Mum was shocked.

"But, Peter, how are we going to survive on less, are they running out of food?" she asked.

Father said "No."

"Then, what has gone wrong?" Mum pleaded. "How come we have so little food?"

Father's reply was unexpectedly simple. He said, "Hunger knows no pride. Hungry ones line the route where we queue up for our rations with outstretched hands, in silence. I could not walk past them without giving them each a little."

Mum burst into tears as she said "But darling, that will not save them. It will add us to their number."

---

[1] The Soviet famine of 1932- 33 killed millions of people in the major grain-producing areas of the Soviet Union, including Ukraine, Northern Caucasus, Volga region, Kazakhstan, the south Urals and west Siberia. It has been estimated that nearly four million died in Ukraine and two million (42% of all Kazakhs) died in Kazakhstan. Stalin and other party members had ordered that kulaks (land-owning peasants) were 'to be liquidated as a class' and so they became a target for the state. They were portrayed by the Bolsheviks as class enemies, which culminated in a Soviet campaign of political repressions, including arrests, deportations and executions of large numbers. Major contributing factors to the famine included the forced collectivisation of agriculture as a part of the Soviet first five-year plan, forced grain procurement, combined with rapid industrialisation, a decreasing agricultural workforce, and several bad droughts.

"I know," Dad said, "but it will save my sanity. I could not walk past them with food in my hands, theirs stretched out to me, swollen from hunger. They looked like something out of space, not human."

How my parents survived that period is nothing short of a miracle. Yes, the queues of starving people grew longer each day, and it was just a matter of days before Dad came home empty-handed. They quickly made the decision to up and go, as to stay was to die. They dressed their three children well against the cold. I was 18 months old, my sister Irma three years old, and my eldest sister Lucya, six. Two children walked, and one had to be carried. Mother's sister and my grandmother completed the little group that walked out of death to life. Miraculously, they made it to the next town.

My mother and her family recovered from their ordeal. There was nothing else for it but to look ahead, never back. Father got a very good position in a large high school, and they had plenty to eat. However, with the *Galadovka* still fresh in their minds, they could not take food for granted. They spent a happy 18 months there. They bought a cow, had chickens and, in the summer, grew vegetables.

My grandmother's health deteriorated during that time, as she developed stomach cancer. It was just a matter of time before she died. My mother felt the blow of her mother's death immensely. She had hardly adjusted to her father's death, not many years earlier, and now her mother, who had been such a tower of strength to her, was also gone.

Her sister Lydia went to university and qualified as an accountant – again a much sought-after profession. She married a handsome officer who was also a professional man, an agricultural scientist, and they seemed happy, for a while anyway. He drank more than was good for him or should I say, for his wife. He became quite aggressive when under the influence and she was often subjected to his anger. He would ask her to take his boots off for him and if she was not quick enough, he would give her a kick. She was so dainty: it was impossible to imagine anyone hurting her. On one such occasion she was pregnant and my mother walked in on the scene. Without uttering a word, she just stood before him, waiting for his explanation. When none came, she walked out again. Apparently, he sobered up instantly and asked his wife's forgiveness. He held my mother and father in very high esteem. The next day he came to my mother and apologised, asking her for forgiveness.

Halfway through 1935, my father was asked to join the Communist Party. When he refused, the NKVD[2] stepped into the picture. He was interrogated three times. They refused to accept his refusal. His plea that he was not interested in politics fell on deaf ears. They needed clever people like him to carry out their repressive system. After the third interrogation, my father knew that his arrest was imminent. Once again, our parents picked us up, threw a few belongings together and were on a train to put as much distance between themselves and the NKVD as possible. It was decided to go all the way to Crimea. Who knew, maybe communism was not as ruthless there, maybe there were still some remaining pockets of humanity acting with honour and a sense of right and wrong. Their hopes were in vain. They had to do something, or Father would have been taken in 1935 and not 1937, as it later turned out.

---

[2] The People's Commissariat for Internal Affairs, abbreviated NKVD, was the interior ministry of the Soviet Union. Established in 1917, the agency was originally tasked with conducting regular police work and overseeing the country's prisons and labour camps. It was disbanded in 1930, only to be reinstated by Joseph Stalin as an all-union commissariat in 1934. The functions of the secret police organisation were transferred to the NKVD in 1934, giving it a monopoly over law enforcement activities that lasted until the end of World War II. The NKVD is known for its role in political repression and for carrying out the Great Purge under Stalin.

On arrival in Crimea, Father had a lot of opportunity to leave his mark on education. He was highly qualified and had excellent references from every school in which he had worked. There was also an acute shortage of good teachers. By 'good teachers' I mean teachers who could not only teach well but also manage the uncontrollable children whose parents had fallen victim to either a purge or starvation.

Throughout the periods of starvation, children lasted longer than adults. A lot of children survived their parents to be so emotionally ruined that they did not respond to learning as normal children did. There were a large number of these children in Russia at that time. These children were emotional cripples, and no one could reach them. Their wellbeing was so battered that they did not respond to the usual methods of communication. Their pain kept life at bay. Father had also studied psychology and had a very positive approach. He knew when to discipline, when to teach and when to nurture, and these children needed all three. Yet, if the dose of any one of these three was wrong it did not work and the children gave the teachers hell. Father had a lot of confidence in the success of his approach.

The school in which Father accepted a position had a large percentage of disturbed children. He saw this as a challenge, but he also thought that if the authorities realised his potential, they might just leave him free a little longer. Twelve months after his commencement at that school, Father was bestowed the highest of awards, a trip to Moscow and the meeting of dignitaries and, of course, the red star.

Chapter 2 – 1937, Crimea

I look at my five-year-old granddaughter and it suddenly dawns on me that I was that very age when my father was taken from me.

Five years old: defenceless, vulnerable, too little to be at the mercy of the Kremlin and the NKVD as it was then. It is mind-boggling to imagine that a five-year-old could survive a fate like that.

It was 1937 when the purge on intellect was carried out and my father was presented with the choice of becoming part of the execution of the purge or to fall victim to it. He became a victim. My mother, in her despair, said many times that if only he had made a different choice, we would still have had him with us. It used to hurt her so much that this sacrifice did not save a single soul, just added one more. It seemed to her such a waste of a very beautiful person, swallowed up by evil.

At the time I could not understand what she was saying, and for me it became more like a jigsaw puzzle, with pieces missing.

Before my parents left Siberia, their beloved homeland, my father had been interrogated three times. This was all part of the NKVD's attempt to have him on 'their team' to execute their plan, the purge. He knew there wouldn't be a fourth time, as that time would be his arrest. Father confronted Mum with this reality, not possibility. The reality of him agreeing to be part of the purge or to be taken.

"For myself I cannot do what is expected of me, but for you and the children I can do the impossible," he said. Mum just shook her head as she dropped into his arms, weeping. They knew that Father would cease to exist once he stepped over the line of his own conscience and became a tool of evil.

I remember looking for my father on that fateful morning, going from room to room and being sure he would turn up to straighten things out and protect us as he always had.

When it happened, I went to bed one night and everything was as beautiful as I was used to in my short life. We followed Mother to milk the cow after our baths, in our nighties, with a glass in our hands for her to fill with milk. We loved watching Mother as she milked while we drank it. We listened to the rhythm of the milk hitting the bucket and were filled with joy and peace. To this day I love milking. We have not had a cow, but a goat has been in our lives for 30-odd years, and I love milking her.

The contrast alone was so horrific. One night all was as it ever was, but the next morning there was complete destruction of everything that made sense and the one person who was always protecting me was gone.

The secret police arrived at 8.00pm and their search for evidence for my father's arrest took six hours. My father was formally arrested at 2.00am. My seven-year-old sister and I slept through the search, but my 11-year-old sister Lucya did not. She heard the strange voices and people shouting in the adjoining room. On seeing the scene, she knew instantly who those strangers were.

She ran to my father, sat on his lap and wept as she cried, "You are not going to take my papa away. I won't let go of him. I won't let him go!"

Six hours later they did take him away, dragging my screaming sister behind them. She was torn away, thrown onto the road as the black car disappeared into the night.

All the males in my father's family had befallen the same fate. They, too, would not betray goodness and truth and, consequently, they were destroyed by the time my father Peter was an adult. The only reason Peter had escaped the same fate earlier was because he was a child during the revolution. Joining the party and becoming 'one of them' was a test he failed, and the price was his life.

In the morning I awoke to a noise I had never heard before: loud weeping, and mumbling words that could not be understood. I called out to my mother, but she did not respond. I froze with fear as this was completely unlike her. I don't know how long I lay there, terrified, but eventually I ventured out of bed and went to look for Mother.

The noise increased as I proceeded to our lounge.

The horrific scene that confronted me was beyond description. All our worldly belongings were thrown in the middle of the room, torn, broken pictures with holes punched through them; some were actually torn out of their frames.

I followed the noise and found my two sisters, but still no mother. I wanted to move, but my legs seemed to belong to someone else, they were certainly not obeying me. Again, I don't know how long I stood there, unable to move. Why were my sisters ignoring me? In fact, it seemed they did not even see me. Most of all, I had to find Dad. He would make everything all right, but where was he?

At some point I did move. I must have, as I found myself in another room and there was Mother, sitting on a chair staring into space, without any sign of life. I approached her gingerly instead of confidently, as had been our pattern. I stood right in front of her, touching her, but without response at all. I wanted to scream, but I also became like a statue, like her, not here, not real. All that I saw had to be a nightmare, just a bad dream from which I would wake any moment and Mum would be standing beside my bed, smiling. I finally collapsed at her feet, but still there was no response. I put her hand on my head and we lay there motionless, like bits of wood.

I began to sob louder and louder; now I, too, was like my sisters.

"Where is my papa?" I screamed, shocking myself with the volume. As I dropped my head on Mum's lap, I suddenly felt a movement on my head. Mum was back. She took my hand in her hands and turned my face to face hers, and she held me for quite some time before starting to drift into her pain again.

All she said was, "My poor, poor children, so little, so little." The other thing she said was, "We are finished, this is the end for the four of us."

When she did come to, she also expressed her grief, but what frightened me the most was when she called out in a loud voice: "My God, my God, *why*?" In Russia at that time no one was allowed to worship God, as communism was supposed to fill our spiritual needs, or part of them, yet I seemed to know that Mum was addressing powers other than human. God surely was present, or we would never have made it through that time.

That day seemed to go on forever and, by the end of the day, we were on the street, not allowed to take with us even the most personal things. It was getting dark, and I can still see the fall of gentle snow as we stood there, not knowing what to do, and then we saw our cow walking towards us, tripping over the rope that hung from her neck. Even the cow was thrown out of the stable, and that seemed to seal our fate. We watched her disappear into the distance, tears flowing for our Maruska.

We looked up and down the street without seeing a soul. Our friends, Father's colleagues, parents of children he had given so much to, were all ruled by fear of the same happening to one of them if they helped us. My father was taken because he would not join the Kremlin in their destruction of all that is noble and good.

We found a deserted house. It was locked, but we managed to get in through the veranda. It was bitterly cold, but at least we were sheltered from the wind. We felt our way into a corner; it was pitch dark by then. We huddled together, both to keep warm and to comfort each other. I did not mind the cold, for Mum was back from wherever she had been before.

"She will know what to do," were my thoughts.

By then I knew that my father had been taken by the NKVD and, even at five years old, I knew that no one returned after being taken by them. Mum was back, though, and holding me in her arms. I can still smell her body, the most beautiful scent in the world, the warmth, the sweetness of her breath: that was the love that saved me.

The days that followed all drifted together into pain and confusion. Mum would go away in the morning and not be back until dark. We saw no one as no one would come near us – they did not dare. At night, once again, we would be huddled together and, next morning, Mum would be gone again.

It was in the middle of the night when Mum started to faint. The first time it happened we thought she was dead. Lucya, aged 11, ran for the doctor while my seven-year-old sister screamed and I froze with fear, blocking my ears and closing my eyes, waiting for my Lucya to return with the doctor. I would sit in the corner by Mum's side, whispering comforting words in her ear and, eventually, she would return to us, and we would try to comfort her with our love. The doctor left, telling Lucya that if it happened again, we should pour a bucket of cold water over her head, as this would bring her to consciousness while she ran for the doctor.

I remember on one such occasion the doctor saying, "Paulina, my little one, if weeping would bring him back, I would weep with you, but you know it won't, your faints are only frightening the children. You are all they have."

We found out later that the NKVD were interrogating my mother, trying to break her spirit so as to get her to denounce my father, condemn him for crimes he did not commit, and have their marriage annulled, freeing her of the stigma of having a husband who was an 'enemy of the people', which was one of the terms they used to describe people like my father. Another was 'political prisoner'.

Part of the interrogations were so simple, yet so cruel. The interrogators would sit eating in front of her, the table laden with beautiful food, every type of tasty dish you can imagine, all the time saying all she had to do was to agree with them and she could sit down and eat and, what's more, she could take all the food she wanted for her hungry children. Oh yes, and she would be honoured by the authorities for her deeds. All this would be published in the *Pravda* newspaper.

But what they did not mention was that this very newspaper would be shown to the prisoner in jail, and they would say to him, "See, even your wife and children see you as an evil man that had to be jailed to protect the community." It was then filed with the rest of their documentation; for sure, they did it all the legal way.

My mother's reply was always, "Never will I say anything bad about this man. He was the most honourable person I had the privilege to know and love."

The interrogators laughed in her face, saying, "Yes, you will! No mother will stand by and let her children starve to death while she can prevent it. Oh yes, you will agree all right!"

I don't know how we made it without our mother giving in. She kept going back to headquarters day after day to apply for work and was interrogated instead, but she did not give in. The fainting at night continued, though. My sister Lucya ran for the doctor while Irma threw a bucket of water over her and I kept on blocking my ears and closing my eyes, only opening them when I heard the doctor's footsteps and his voice saying, "Paulinchen, Paulinchen, you are getting weaker and weaker by the minute. How long can you last?"

She would shake her head and say, "I'd sooner die than to do a terrible thing like that."

"But what about the children?" the doctor continued. "It is not fair that they should die because you could do no evil or, worse still, have the state pick them up and brainwash them into being communists believing their parents were evil. Think about it. It is not fair, and they are too little to sacrifice!"

Mother would just shake her head and say, "I can't do it. I can't do it."

"Paulinchen, Paulinchen, think again!"

I can still see my mother sitting on the floor, soaking wet, her waist-long hair trailing down her back and over her face. She looked so fragile, so in need of someone to look after her, yet, somehow, deep within herself, she seemed to find unlimited strength. On seeing us so upset, she would quickly pick herself up and come to us with arms outstretched. She would weep for a while, but as our weeping increased, hers subsided and she would stop to comfort us into the oblivion of sleep, if you can call that kind of experience 'sleep'. When traumatised to the degree we were, sleep was no escape, it all followed us in our slumber.

After an endless chain of interrogations by the NKVD, my mother ran out of strength and collapsed on her way home and a train nearly cut her in half. She had no memories of it at all. The engine driver risked his own life by picking her up. Towns around us had heard of the woman who was not going to give in to NKVD, so the engine driver knew who she was and dropped her off at our railway station, saying, "I believe she belongs to you."

People present just stared at him, too frightened to utter a sound and baffled by this man's actions. He truly was putting his own life on the line helping a person who had stood up to the NKVD. Not many would.

In fact, only one person out of the whole town responded, though in a limited way, to our plight and only during the night. She would suddenly appear out of the darkness with food, but she had six children of her own to feed single-handedly and food was always a scarce commodity in Russia. It was quite common for a whole town to die of starvation with no one coming to its rescue. So effective was the Kremlin's brainwashing of the world, that no one believed that what they saw was actually happening – a bit like it was with Bosnia and the Serbs, the atrocities have desensitised the world. Confusion sets in and people hold back because the path to compassion is fogged up with misinformation.

My mother, my sisters and I reached a point knowing that all that was to be done was completed, all that was left was to keep still, not move, not try to improve things, not even think, just keep still. And yet, the love which bound us together, I have never again experienced since. It seemed as if God Himself held us in His arms. The four of us held each other so closely that there was no space between us, just a oneness, an entity that had four hearts beating. I felt my mother's warm breath on my neck. I smelled her body – the feeling was so overpowering that none of us wanted it to end and we only wanted to move on just like that into the next life. We were all sure that we were about to die, but had no dread of it, no more fear of the unknown, just perfect peace and acceptance of whatever was about to happen. The best part was that Mum would never again leave us or faint.

How long we were in this state I will never know as time became irrelevant. Light followed darkness, night followed day, and that was all we were aware of.

Then, one evening, a knock on the door startled us. None of us moved, but the knocking persisted until the door was thrown open. A woman entered the room, addressing someone behind her and then she spoke to my mother. She lit a candle, held it in front of her in search of something, until she spotted us. She froze in her steps and said nothing for a while, just stared at us. It was strange. The little candlelight hurt our eyes and then she spoke, screaming at the person behind her.

"Look what your precious party has done to these people," she yelled. "You are a monster to be part of such cruelty."

We found out later the person she was yelling at was her mother, who was a member of the Communist Party.

"What have they done to you?" she continued. "My God, how could anyone but a monster do this to others?"

Once again, I closed my eyes and blocked my ears and wished with all my heart that the woman would go away, but no, she persisted, addressing my mother by her first name.

"Paulina, you have to get out of this hell, if not for yourself, then for the three little ones," she said, "What will happen to them if you die?"

She was shouting by now, and I felt my mother's body go rigid and fear grasped me. I hung on to her even tighter, but could not speak, just wished this woman would go away and leave us alone. The peace we had felt was disintegrating before our eyes. Please, please, make her go away, I pleaded in my heart as I could not utter a sound.

She left, but she returned next morning with a form in her hand, pleading with my mother to go to the authorities and ask to be employed.

"So you can feed your children," she said. "Please, please, come with me. You will not be interrogated. That is finished, but you must go and ask for work. It's the only way, Paulina."

And that was how we did not perish after all. Not many people could stand up to the NKVD, as most women crumbled. The interrogations were such that very few could defy them the way my mother did, but then, as she said, she just could not do what was demanded of her.

"It's that simple," she would say. "Some things are beyond you."

She never saw herself as a martyr, or an extraordinary person, as I see her now. She would say repeatedly, "I am no different from any other ordinary person," and that she just did her best under extremely difficult circumstances. That's all.

I was shattered that day when my mother, with the help of the other woman, left us. I was sure I would never see her again. She looked so frail, as even her body size seemed to have shrunk to a child's size. If the woman had not physically supported her, I am sure she could not have walked away as she did. The woman almost carried her.

I wanted to scream, "Please, please, come back Mum!" But nothing came out of my mouth. It just opened and shut, without making a sound.

Our peace was broken, and we were fragmented once again. No one knew where we were going, and Mum was gone once again. I curled up in the corner, closed my eyes and waited, not knowing what it was I was waiting for.

My mother was accepted into the workforce and the interrogations stopped. It was the woman who had come to us who had convinced the authorities that my mother was finished, so if they did not want three more children orphaned, they'd better stop, so that she might recover and support them.

My mother was employed by the collective farm, and the state took we three children into long day care and school.

Once Mother was accepted into the *kolkhoz*[3] (collective farm) workforce, the interrogations stopped. Mother became one of the women she had felt so sorry for before Father was taken. She had watched them being brought to the nursery on the back of a truck to feed their babies, standing, not sitting down, with 'cardboard dresses' as Mother used to call them. The milk from their breasts soaked their clothing, then dried, got wet again, and dried again, until the fronts of their dresses were as stiff as cardboard. How their breasts must have hurt, as most of them had no bras. They would be running to their babies, holding their breasts, so as to have a little more time with the infants. That was their lunch break, and they ate little sandwiches or plain bread, while feeding their babies. Then it was back to the truck, leaving their babies in the hands of strangers who had more children than they could care for in a loving, personal way. Some mothers cried as they left and the truck would take them back to the fields, to hew, plant or harvest. Most work on the land was done by hand, not machinery.

Mum said she often used to weep as she watched them from a distance. She used to say to Father how unfair it was that they should suffer like that, and now she had become one of them, except we children were no longer babies.

---

[3] A *kolkhoz* was a form of collective farm in the Soviet Union. *Kolkhozes* existed along with state farms, or *sovkhoz*. These were the two components of the socialized farm sector that began to emerge in Soviet agriculture after the October Revolution of 1917. The 1920s were characterised by a spontaneous emergence of collective farms, under the influence of travelling propaganda workers. Initially a collective farm resembled an updated version of the traditional Russian 'commune', the generic 'farming association', and finally the *kolkhoz*. This gradual shift to collective farming gathered momentum during the forced collectivisation campaign that began in 1928 as means to opposing counterrevolutionary elements.
During the Stalinist period, a *kolkhoz* member received a share of the farm's product and profit according to the number of days worked. In addition, the *kolkhoz* was required to sell its grain crop and other products to the state at fixed prices. These were set very low by Soviet government, and the difference between what the state paid the farm and what the State charged consumers represented a major source of income for the Soviet government.

Mother's days at the kolkhoz would start before daybreak and end after dark. I remember waiting for her after returning from kindergarten, sitting on the doorstep, getting more and more tired. At first, I was certain I was waiting in vain and thought I would never see Mum again. I would often fall into a slumber only to wake to my mother's gentle hands picking me up and carrying me to somewhere more comfortable, while she whispered, "Dinner won't be long. I will make something that you really like." I was in heaven, Mum was back.

As time passed, I realised that as long as Mother was alive, she would come back but the spectre of something happening to her, just as it did to Father, never left me. We soon found out the hard way what happened to Father, particularly my two older sisters, who were taunted to the extreme at school.

"Your father is an enemy of the people. He is in jail where he belongs!" At first my sisters tried to defend Dad, but then they realised that even children were trying to please the authorities in the hope of not losing their own fathers. When I heard anything like that I just disappeared out of their sight. I became quite good at finding nooks to hide in and came out only when they were gone. Fortunately, no one in charge at the nursery missed me as they all had more children than they could care for comfortably. This became my salvation: hide and block your ears if you have to, don't listen, it is too hurtful. How could people change so suddenly from receiving help from my father and showing him tremendous respect and gratitude to saying the opposite in just a matter of days or weeks? These were confusing thoughts for me at that time. How could a five-year-old untangle this web of wrongs?

In later years, my mother told me many accounts of her experiences at that time, but they are often disjointed as she frequently could not complete a segment of her history before it became too painful. I never asked her any questions when I saw that it was hurting her to recall events, so I have accounts of certain occasions in snippets that I cannot always put into a coherent perspective.

One such experience she related was when she started hewing row after row to rid the plants of weeds. The foreman would come up to her and try to show her how it was done, but she kept injuring her feet and they were badly cut. He addressed her as he had always done, with respect. He would say, "Madame Gerzen, if you stopped crying you would be able to see better and therefore dodge your feet."

Like the doctor before him, he would say, "If weeping could bring your husband back, I would weep the longest as I admired your husband no end. He helped my son to get through with high marks, but it will change nothing. He is gone, you are not likely to see him ever again and three little children are depending on you for survival."

Then he taught Mother how to hew without chopping her feet and toes, or the plants.

All around her people swore, male and female alike. That's how they vented their frustration and anger. Mum's reaction was of shock.

They laughed and said, "You wait and see, this way of living will numb all your sensitivities and you will become just like us, angry and lashing out at something, even if it is only by swearing. There is no point in niceties, this is a battle for survival."

Mum never got used to the swearing, and she felt very sad that excessively hard work and depravation of all niceties had made those women so hard and cynical.

Mother made contact with her younger sister, Lydia, whom she had brought into adulthood as her parents died quite young, in their early 60s. Mother was more like a mother to her than a sister. She had educated her, too, and her sister was now an accountant. Lydia was married by now, with two children, yet, on hearing of my mother's plight, she and her husband boarded a train in a matter of days.

We were all overjoyed. At last, we would no longer be 'lepers' or have abuse thrown at us. We would be with someone who loved us and knew the full story. It was so overwhelming that we could hardly speak. Our feelings were of pure relief. I think we were afraid of collapsing into a heap, but instead we just looked at each other not daring to give voice to what was inside us.

The next day Mum said, "We will be all right now."

Only 16 months earlier my parents had done the same thing, leaving their beloved Siberia in the hope of escaping the destruction of communism. Their hope was that communism wasn't as evil throughout all of Russia. How wrong they were. Russian communism was the fastest-growing cancer and its tentacles reached long distances and destroyed all in its path, except for its law enforcers. It lasted 72 years before it burnt itself out, leaving in its wake the total destruction of more than 60 million people, according to Aleksandr Solzhenitsyn.

The arrival of my mother's sister and her husband was our salvation. Not only did we now have someone to love and be loved by, but we were no longer isolated, and they made a lot of practical changes. They were appalled at the treatment we had suffered at the hands of the town.

The first thing we did was to leave that town and make a new start.

We soon settled into our new community. My aunt, being an accountant, had no trouble finding work. Her husband was an agricultural scientist, and he also had many options. Both my uncle and aunt found work very quickly. Mother stayed at home and cared for the children, five of us. It was pure joy. Nonetheless, the cloud of Dad's tragic disappearance followed us in everything we did. Time did not seem to heal, but we were a family.

Mother was seen as a widow. It hurt her to deny Dad, but we knew there was no other way, and we just never talked about him. During that time Mother also did a lot of sewing, not because there wasn't enough income, but because you could not buy the necessary food. She sewed for women who worked in collective restaurants, for the elite, in exchange for food.

It seemed as though we were heading for yet another *Galadovka* starvation. The stores were empty. Sometimes she sewed until midnight or until her brother-in-law would jump out of bed and remove the globe from its socket saying, "Don't I work hard enough to provide for you that you have to work instead of sleep?" She explained to him her reasons, that all the food needed for the family could not be bought and that she got paid with food. He must have been so frustrated as he really wanted to provide for Mum and us. He, too, was terribly shocked about my father's fate. He knew Dad well and admired and respected him immensely. He also knew that Father could have made a different choice but did not.

On other nights, Mother would stand in queues for bread only to come back in the morning empty-handed.

"Never mind," she would say. "I only missed out by about half a dozen, so tonight I will go earlier and get to the counter before they run out of bread. Just have a glass of milk for now."

Once again we had a cow we named Maruska after the cow we had lost on that fatal day in 1937 and that 'glass of milk' really saved us. It helped us to survive that particular time with so little food. This was 1939. No one knew the cause of the extreme shortage of food. There was no failure of harvest, no drought; the grain just went elsewhere.

We did have a good year, the year before the commencement of World War II, after Mum remarried. There was plenty to eat then.

Mother met this beautiful man who was working with her brother-in-law and was also an agricultural scientist. He instantly fell in love with Mum. He had lost his wife and children to *Galadovka* less than two years before and thought he would never be able to come to terms with his loss, until he met my mother. Mum's reaction to him was simple. She had no idea how she would feel if she was not 'dead inside', as she put it. He knew exactly what she meant, but said to her that he had enough love to cover her, her children and the whole world. This is how people in love feel, particularly if they have suffered as he had. He pleaded with Mum to give him a chance to prove his love and earnestness.

Mother married him, retaining her own name and throwing we children into confusion and new pain: that of being unable to comprehend how all this was possible. Dad could well be alive and suffering in hell and now Mum had another man in her life and bed. Our mother, a saint in our eyes and our whole world, was only human, so had let another man into her life to take Father's place. We were shocked. We were sure we would lose Mum as we could never be part of 'that man', as we called him. Children only see things in extremes: something is either right or wrong, black or white, and there is no in between. At the same time, we did have three very different reactions to this development.

My eldest sister Lucya, who was nearly 14, saw it as wrong. She felt Mum was betraying Dad, who had forsaken his life rather than do wrong. How could Mum betray someone so noble? My middle sister, Irma, who was barely 10, simply told Mum she was just as hurt as Lucya and just as confused, but that she trusted her judgement completely and told her that if this man was going to care for us, she would accept him and even call him Dad. I was amazed at her attitude. She was only 18 months older than me and yet, she had answers, where I did not.

I was nearly nine and waiting for the confusion to disappear. I also trusted Mum, but nothing fitted; nothing made sense. I just avoided him like the plague. I stayed outside as long as possible and went to bed really early, soon after he got home from work. My aim was not to be confronted by him. I developed quite a technique. Lucya stayed away for a whole year with our aunt and just came for visits when Mum was alone.

I once overheard 'this man' say to Mum, "Why are the girls avoiding me?" But I think he knew why: we just could not cope with him taking Father's place. Also, not knowing whether Dad was dead or alive kept the door of hope wide open for we three girls. We felt that one day he would come back, and this man seemed to shatter all our little illusions. Mum often told us he was not trying to take Father's place, as no one could ever do that.

To my eldest sister's accusations, she simply replied, "Let your father be the judge, not you. You of all people should know how much I loved your father, and I always will. You also know what it took not to betray him by denouncing him. You are just a child, that is why you don't understand how life can be."

The village we had moved to was only three kilometres from our previous town. My stepfather's work was in rural districts.

Stepfather very much wanted to have a child of his own, maybe to replace the children he lost to starvation in 1935 in the Ukraine, or maybe he just loved Mum so much that he wanted to bond with a child. Mum was not so sure, but she eventually agreed. He reasoned it would bring us together as a family and that we girls would no longer see him as an outsider, and he was right. Mother gave birth to a little boy in 1940. His name was Yuri, but we always referred to him as 'Malchick', meaning 'little boy'. He brought us together as a family. The strange thing was that he looked just like our father, with curly blond hair, the biggest blue eyes and a beautiful expression on his little face, peaceful and loving. We adored him from the moment we set eyes on him, so how could we now ignore his father? A miracle did happen.

We girls could not get enough of him. He had four mothers, not one. It was just as well that we had to go to school or none of us would have done anything useful. We just could not tear ourselves away from him. When Mum nursed him, we crowded around him, forming a circle and looking at him adoringly. Eventually she had to send us away as he was alternating between sucking and looking at us.

We began our slow journey towards loving his father, our stepfather. As it turned out, it was not hard at all. He was kind to us and Mum and we had a little brother, his child, who went from loving arm to loving arm and back to Mum to be fed. Mum asked us to disappear or she would sit there all day trying to feed him as he kept letting go of her nipple while looking around at us. We would withdraw reluctantly. We had a wonderful eight months or so. Mum was peaceful, and we had not seen her like that since Father was taken.

Spring 1941 changed everything as World War II began for Russia. Not many days later an order came from Stalin that all the people of German descent were to be interned in Siberia. Our ancestry went back to 1750, which made no difference. We were identified as German, and we had to be interned.

We were given 24 hours in which to present ourselves at the nearest train station. Our stepfather was instantly enlisted as he was an officer.

We were told to take sufficient food for at least two weeks. Mum and all the other women went into a frenzy of cooking and baking. Mum cooked a whole lot of pork and layered it with fat as a preservative as, when desperate, this could be eaten as well, bread or no bread. We all knew we could not possibly carry two weeks' worth of supplies. Mum could hardly carry all the things the baby needed. *Galadovka* was not just a theory, it was a stark reality to Mum, having gone through it twice in her short life. She had no doubt of its inevitability if we did not bring enough food with us. Accordingly, she packed many bundles and bags for each of us to carry.

In a matter of days, we were on our way to the nearest railway station, and so, it seemed, was half of the Crimean population. The station was not all that far away, but it took us nearly half a day to reach it on foot, mainly because there were so many people heading in the same direction. Crimea had a very high percentage of people of German ancestry, not to mention the mixed families where one parent was German and the other Russian. The entire population seemed to be on the move. It was a hot spring day, and children got sunstruck as well as sunburnt.

Our stepfather caught up with us at the railway station. He was distraught to see us in this state, especially his son, our baby Malchick.

"How can they do this to me?" he cried. "I am an officer about to defend my country, and my wife and son are going to be interned. Darling, I will fight the authorities tooth and nail until they let me go, at least until you reach your destination."

As he said this, I am sure he knew the folly of it, as we all knew they would not let an officer go.

For the first time, we saw our stepfather as someone special, someone who would take care of us, if at all possible, someone who was part of us instead of an intruder, but why now and not before, we thought. We would never get a chance to show him our love and appreciation for what he had already done for us. We felt terrible about it and, when he hugged our little boy, we all broke into tears.

"I will be back," he kept saying. "I will be back, even if I have to desert." This gave Mum more of a shock than comfort as deserters were shot on the spot. But there was no time to hold on to any thought or idea. Next thing, he was gone.

The railway station was so full of people that no one could sit down. As far as the eye could see there were crying, inconsolable people, including weeping children. It seemed like an ocean of sobbing faces, and as if they were all disembodied. Cattle trains came, filled with folk, and moved on, only to be replaced by another train to load with people. There seemed to be an endless supply of people – the more the train took away, the more there seemed to be. New arrivals came in bigger numbers than what the trains were able to take.

It was so utterly and terribly sad, particularly when families had to be split: the Russian part stayed and the German part went. In some cases, people had to be torn from those who had to board, running after the train – it was a terrible sight. When a train moved, some fell on the track and were cut down by the next train. Worst of all was when people refused to let go of their loved ones and ran with them when the train was already moving until they were dragged along, then fell to the ground. People lay down along the track until guards came along and removed them.

It was like a conveyor belt without end. As one train moved out, another took its place. The same scene kept repeating itself over and over again. It was heartbreaking. We all seemed to be in a horrific nightmare from which there was no waking, like trying to get out of quicksand: the more one moved, the deeper the hole became. You look for someone's firm hand to pull you out, but there is none. All of humanity seemed to be in the same position, drowning in the quicksand of war and destruction.

Somehow, we managed to find Mum's sister Lydia and her little ones. Her husband, too, was Russian and an officer. Like my stepfather, he had to report the same day the war had started. When he heard that his wife and children were on the way to Siberia, he was furious. How could they do this to him? Didn't he prove himself loyal by volunteering? Somehow, he too found us before we boarded the train. He was so distraught that he was also willing to desert. It took my aunt quite some time to convince him that there had to be a better way, through legal channels. As it turned out, there weren't any and he later deserted anyway.

Before dark, we finally got on the train. We tried so hard to be in the same carriage, and we managed to. They put so many people into one carriage that not many could squat down. Most people had to stand, and only we children squatted, with Mum and Aunt Lydia standing over us protectively. Our little Malchick seemed to know that something terrible was happening, as he did not cry like babies do; he just looked at Mum with his big blue eyes and tears just ran down his face.

That got us all going until Mum said, "Please, girls, try to look happy and he will stop too." It worked and Mum's breast did the rest and he fell asleep.

The frightful feeling of despair was felt by everyone. What were they going to do with us? Stories started to circulate of other trains being blown up by aircraft dropping bombs. No one knew if this was done by Germans or Russians, not that it really mattered, and then someone suggested that someone climb on top of the carriage and write in German, *'This train is full of German people on their way to Siberia'*. All adults could write in German: Russian is so different that you had to be German to be able to write in German. That idea saved our lives. The person climbing up and writing risked his own life, but it worked. We heard heavy planes loaded with bombs circling over us. We hoped they would protect us from our enemies, the Russians. We did not know how they could, but it felt good that there was someone there who cared and knew what was happening to us.

Chapter 3 – 1941, Caucasus

The train did not stop all night. Then, as dawn broke, it did stop for a short time. People spilled out of the carriage to relieve themselves, but no one dared to go too far from the train in case it moved without warning, so modesty had to be put aside. However, people were still left behind every time the train stopped, children were lost, or mothers, as the train moved on without warning.

During the second night of our journey, the train suddenly stopped and all passengers were ordered to disembark. The train was needed for the Russian war effort and that was what saved us from going all the way to Siberia.

We were in Caucasus[4], and made our way to the station's waiting room. The air raids must have already reached that region, judging by the glass-less windows. It was a very cold and windy night. We huddled together for warmth and comfort and waited until morning. At dawn it got colder still. As soon as it was light enough, we made our way to the town itself, which was a fair distance from the station. On reaching it, we realised it was not a big one, but it did look fairly orderly. When we came to the town square, we found a bench and sat there while Aunt Lydia went to the authorities to report and identify us. On finding out her profession, once again she was instantly offered employment.

And now came the difficult part: where were we going to live? At the end of a long search, Mum and Aunt Lydia found a single room in an old house belonging to a widow. She was a local, quite dark and spoke almost no

---

[4] The Caucasus is a region between the Black and the Caspian seas and mainly occupied by Armenia, Azerbaijan, Georgia and parts of southern Russia. It is home to the Caucasus Mountains, including the Greater Caucasus mountain range, which has historically been considered a natural barrier between eastern Europe and western Asia.

Russian. This was a town that had managed to cling to its roots despite the Kremlin and the communists' way of stripping everyone of their identity and dignity. The communists took all the material things from people, but not always their identity, not yet anyway. Caucasus natives had yet to learn their terrorists' language. I think they may have been Muslim and were exceptionally clean, despite their poverty.

My mother and her sister sat down and talked. Aunty could not possibly feed us all, so they had to look at alternatives and came up with a solution, but it meant we had to part from each other. In a village five kilometres away a kindergarten director was needed, and Mum had that kind of training and was accepted after applying for the job. My two sisters stayed with our Aunt Lydia as there was no high school in the village, and they helped to look after her little ones.

So Mum, baby Malchick and I went to the little village where Mum had employment. We had one room with one bed and a Russian stove called a *petchka* which provided heat. It was fed with straw or any kind of scrub for fuel.

In Caucasus, the climate was mild. In fact they had no stables for their animals, which just stayed in their little yards to which they were brought at the end of each day to be milked and fed by hand. In the morning after milking, they were let out to pasture. In the summer there was a lot of scrub growth, which was wonderful fuel for the *petchka*, lasted much longer than straw and gave a lot more heat, but we had to collect it and bring it home. It was called *buryan*.

We were now in a village where no one spoke our languages, German or Russian. Mum spoke German, but we children had forgotten our German as we were not allowed to speak it. At some point in Soviet history all speaking of foreign languages was forbidden. Our first language was German but, from the time our grandmother died, we were no longer allowed to speak it. Only one person in the entire village spoke Russian, and he was the head of it.

I think the people were of Turkish background and they lived very traditionally, quite differently to Russians, or Germans for that matter. We children were fascinated by their customs, such as cooking in the earth, which was a bit like a camp oven in the outback, and going to the forest to relieve themselves. There was not even a 'dunny in the backyard', just a long walk, out of sight. They carried a little urn full of water, as in Aladdin's stories, as they did observe personal hygiene, but differently from our culture.

They ground their own flour between large flat stones with a hole in the middle to feed the wheat into, and another at the bottom where the ground flour came out. It was a very arduous and time-consuming process. For bread, they had big iron pans with lids the same weight. A fire was lit and burnt to coal and it was into this that they put the pan – actually, they dug a hole and buried it. This was how they made their bread, and it was beautiful.

Not having a mutual language, though, completely isolated us from them. They were very strict Muslims, and we could hear them at sunrise and sunset when they called out their prayers in loud voices, kneeling on mats facing Mecca. Their race was called Nagaizi[5], but I don't know much about them.

---

[5] The name used by Lina for this group of people cannot be verified. There were significant Muslim territories in both the Crimea and Caucasus at the onset of WWII, and Nazi Germany saw them as strategically important, promoting a military alliance with them against the Soviet Union. During World War II, particularly in 1943-'44, the Soviet government conducted a series of deportations to Siberia and the central Asian republics. Collaboration with Nazi Germany was cited as the official reason for the operation, but this has been disputed by accusations of ethnic cleansing against the USSR. The Crimean Tatars, Chechens, Ingushs, Balkars, Karachays, and Meskhetian Turks were some of the groups which were deported, all being predominantly Muslim. Severe loss of life resulted during and after these deportations.

Back at the little room with our *petchka* and a bed, Malchick and I spent almost four seasons. Mum's position in this village was very demanding. She was in charge of 50 children from 6.00am to 6.00pm and had only one assistant. The children had breakfast, morning and afternoon tea, lunch and dinner, so when their parents picked them up they were ready for bed. The food supplies were not all delivered. Buckets of milk had to be picked up every morning, and bread and meals had to be cooked. In warm weather, Malchick and I could join Mum and the children and went home late afternoon, not long before Mum. That was wonderful, but my education had to be put on hold, for two reasons: the main one being our little brother, who was not allowed to be with Mum at the kindergarten and needed looking after; the second reason was that the nearest school was too far away for me to walk to and, besides that, it was during a war. Who cared about the children's education when it was not even certain we would survive? First things first and survival was certainly the priority.

Summer went by quickly. One day my middle sister Irma came to visit. She had walked the five kilometres from the village where she lived with my Aunt Lydia, a long journey. She had been missing Mum terribly and felt that the only way to reach her was to walk. By the time she reached us she was sunburned and dehydrated, and Mum was shocked to see that she had made the long journey all by herself, without even telling my aunt where she was going.

The following winter, Irma made the journey again, this time with three young children in tow. At one point she saw a wolf in the middle of the road. She had seen it a long way off, but had no choice but to stay on the road if she was to get to us. She prayed the animal would not be hungry because, if it was, it would kill them. The little one on Irma's hip started whimpering loudly as they approached the wolf. Irma tried to stop him making any noise, but he was too afraid, so she covered his eyes with her hand as she cuddled him and kept walking very, very slowly. She was close enough to look the wolf in the eye before it stood up and went into the scrub. For a while they ran to put some distance between themselves and the wolf. It was a miracle that it did not attack them. She was so little, certainly not big enough to frighten a wolf.

Irma was so exhausted and shaken by the experience that, on arrival, she just sat on the floor with the three children around her. My sister tried not to cry while we waited for Mum to come home from work. Mum could not believe her eyes when she saw my sister with the children. On seeing Mum, Irma burst into tears and later told Mum the reason for this dangerous journey.

Our uncle had deserted. The Germans were due to occupy their village at any moment, but the Russians were still in charge – even though they disappeared every night, the daytime was still theirs. Our uncle had arrived in the middle of the night only to find that the Russians were still there. My aunt nearly died of shock. He quickly hid under the bed. At first light, my sister and her cousins were packed off to our village and Aunt Lydia locked the room while she went to work. She had to get some food for him without arousing suspicion, then get home after dark when no one was allowed any form of light at all and hope that no one would come to the door while she was home.

In the dark of the night, under the bed, they comforted each other and ate. It was not safe to be in the room as, at any time Soviet soldiers who patrolled the streets could shine a torch into any area they thought looked suspicious. Aunty and Uncle could not talk, or even whisper, as that could betray them, as she was meant to be on her own. How they coped I don't know, but the alternative was a firing squad for him or for both of them.

As I remember it

It was another two weeks before the Germans arrived, and Uncle could get out from under the bed: two weeks of hell. There was no telephone, no transport of any kind, just their legs. Uncle came to pick up his children and to see us, of course. Irma went back with him as Mum could not feed her as well as us and, besides, Aunty could not do without her. More to the point, the children could not do without my sister. They had bonded so closely with her that she had become their 'Mum'. She was the one who nurtured and comforted them, who wiped away their tears when they were sad. Children cannot bond by remote control. They know who the mother is, but it is the one who is close at hand, who comforts, who becomes the 'real' mother.

Irma adored them, and they adored her. When the three-year-old fell sick, it was she who carried him in her arms through the night, not his mother, even though she wanted to do so. He wanted Irma and she loved nurturing him. After all, she was their substitute mother while their actual mother was at work for very long hours. They hardly ever saw Aunt Lydia. Of course, they knew who she was, but they needed a nurturer for as much time as possible.

The three-year-old died in my sister's arms. She carried him while other people went for help. He seemed to be on fire and pointed to his mouth. She wet his lips and tried to give him a drink, but he could not swallow. He had diphtheria and had choked to death by the time help came. She refused to let go of him and just pressed him close to her chest and kept saying, "He will come back. He will come back."

She whispered to him, "Vovchik, Vovchik, I have got you, you can't leave me."

Finally, she had to accept that he was dead, while she had to find a way of healing and letting him go. As she stood there, paralysed with grief, she heard a little whimper at her feet. She looked down and saw the youngest holding onto her leg and crying. He was nearly two, but could not walk. There was just not enough suitable food for little ones. They could not chew ground wheat or even bread. They needed milk, eggs and fruit, of course, and there was none, so he was very weak. He would just slide on his bottom or wait until someone picked him up. Instinctively, Irma picked him up. He sat on her hip and clung to her neck. Yes, Vova was gone, but this one was here, and his needs were enormous. She sought solace in her grief by giving love. The little one was called Yura.

We had arrived in the Caucasus village early in August, a month and a half after the start of World War II. With Russia, the war started in June 1941, and we were on our way to Siberia a week later. Our train journey had been very slow because of the fast-moving front. No one really resisted the Germans as this was the first opportunity for people in Russia to rid themselves of communism. The exceptions were the law enforcers, the hardcore communists – they had a lot to lose as they lived like kings at the expense of the majority.

One summer's day the Germans arrived at our village on their beautiful shiny motorbikes, and not a shot was fired. The population was elated at the retreat of the Russians – not that they knew anything of the Nazi ideology, but they saw this as an opportunity to rid Russia of communism. History books don't tell us about people such as General Vlasov[6], who took his whole division to the German side, just to fight communism, which was like a malignant cancer. All but the law enforcers and party members knew what *Galadovka* was:

---

[6] Andrey Andreyevich Vlasov was a Red Army general. During World War II, he fought in the Battle of Moscow and was later captured attempting to lift the siege of Leningrad. After being captured, he defected to Nazi Germany and headed the Russian Liberation Army (ROA). At the war's end, he changed sides again and ordered the ROA to aid the Prague uprising against the Germans. He and the ROA then tried to escape to the Western Front but were captured by Soviet forces. Vlasov was tried for treason and hanged.

starvation. The people also knew what a purge was, and that they had nothing left to lose and hoped the Germans would help them to build a new Russia. Those were the feelings of the people when the Germans moved in. I say 'moved in' as there was no opposition, no fighting back.

The winter of 1941 in Caucasus arrived early and was much more severe than usual. It was the coldest winter in living memory. Cattle were dying from lack of shelter.

Our little boy and I were completely confined to the one little room with the *petchka*. Mum went to work in darkness and returned in darkness. On returning, she had to go into a field to collect *buryan* for our *petchka*. The house our little room was in was the very last house in the village, so Malchick and I watched her disappear into the darkening distance as we sat by the window. She would gather as she went along, tying it together until she had enough for our *petchka*. She would disappear out of sight and the little one would tense up, grind his little teeth and hang on to me. We did not like seeing the little speck disappearing into the night.

We felt utterly alone in this world. After all, I was only 10 and had experienced the force of evil. There was no theorising, no power of thought that could help wipe it out or even minimise reality. I knew what could happen. What happened to Dad could happen to Mum. We sat at that window like statues, not moving, until we saw that speck reappear. Only then were we sure of Mother's return.

Other times the speck seemed quite close and then suddenly disappeared, and that really frightened us. We later learned the reason for this: she had walked into a snow-covered ditch and then had to crawl out of it with the *buryan* on her back and the wind to contend with. She made it, however. Not once or twice, but throughout the entire winter. The heat of the *petchka* only lasted 24 hours, so every day it had to be relit and heated.

On arriving home, Mum would bring the *buryan* into the little room from which the *petchka* was lit. She would sit, unable to move her fingers, which were so frozen that they were like bits of wood sticking straight out from in front of her hand. The little one was so excited he wanted Mum to hold him, but it took quite some time for me to 'unspell' Mum. So I would unbutton Mum's coat and slip our little boy inside her clothing, where he would find Mum's nipple and settle down. I then warmed Mum up, starting by blowing warm air onto her hands, stroking ever so gently until she felt life returning to them. I then would take off her snowy boots and undo the rest of the buttons of her coat.

Putting *buryan* into the stove was not easy as the wood was quite prickly, with little sticks breaking and scratching our hands and arms. By that time, Mum would have thawed enough and would take over while I held the little one. He would not let Mum out of his sight, constantly making noises and whimpering, like an insecure puppy.

Once the *petchka* was lit, it warmed the room and passage very quickly. Watching it burn was a beautiful sight, and knowing that a meal would be cooked and that the *petchka* would stay hot for the next 24 hours was wonderful. We were safe for a day and Mum would not leave us until the morning.

I felt so sorry for my mother, with her hands red and swollen. I wanted to take them in my hands and somehow make them better. I wanted to put them on my face, as she often held my face in her hands. I wanted to kiss them better, but all I could do was to watch her and hold on to my brother. Once Mother busied herself preparing the meal, it all seemed like magic and she looked very peaceful which had the same effect on me and even more on the little one. He was so tuned in to feelings that nothing escaped him, which pulled Mum and me up no end as his eyes filled with tears very quickly on seeing Mum or me upset.

The vigils that my little brother and I kept in this little room, most of the time on top of the *petchka* as it was the only way we could keep warm, were long and very lonely. At daybreak we watched Mum disappear into the dark and, at the end of the day, we welcomed her back again in semi-darkness, after 12 hours of waiting. At the end of the day there was her disappearance into the distance and darkness again, which we never got used to. Every time she left us to collect *buryan*, our hearts sank. We were sure we would never see her again. After all, wolves were very hungry in winter, and it was very dangerous.

Our two hearts beat as one, but Malchick's beat at twice the pace. He would sit on my lap, his little legs around my waist and his arms around my neck and keep still until we saw a speck coming closer that eventually became Mum. Upon her arrival, the excitement, the pattern, did not vary. He would jump up and down trying to get to Mum. Once he was slipped into Mum's clothing he would not let go until it was safe and the room warm, Mum minus her heavy clothing. Then and only then would he let go of her, because he knew she would not leave us and he would settle down. After all, he was still a long way from being one year old and a lot of confusing things were happening around him.

Towards the end of that winter, Mum discovered that I was suffering from malnutrition. Neither of us felt it coming, but soon I could not walk anymore or hold myself up straight. Mum was so distraught that she went to the head of the village and presented him with the news.

He replied, very surprisingly, "You are feeding 50 children every day. All you have to do is to take a little and you can feed two more."

Mum was furious and said, "You mean to tell me that working 12 hours a day is not enough to feed two children and I have to steal for them? I will not steal from other children. I have more than earned the keep of my two children, so you better find a way."

He knew that being under German occupation, all she had to do was to go to the authorities and lodge a complaint, and he certainly did not want her to do that. He was already walking a tightrope, as a communist who stayed behind, so he truly had to prove himself. His reasons were his people. They would have been devastated and lost had he left them, as he was their leader in every way and their mouthpiece as no one else could speak German. The Germans trusted him, but watched him very closely, just the same.

Mum left it up to him to find a way and he did. At regular intervals, a billy of milk, a large loaf of bread and sometimes even eggs were left at our door. It was wonderful to eat when you were hungry instead of having to wait for hours or a whole day before being able to eat. Best of all was Mum's concern for me and her extra love and attention. I never had any doubt about her love, but to see it expressed and to see her fight to keep me alive was a really special experience.

Towards the end of winter, Mum sent a message for my eldest sister, Lucya, to come and help us through the next winter. She came, but wept over her lost opportunity for an education, as she loved learning new things. At school she was always at the top for academic achievement, and she would have gone a long way had she been born in a different part of the world. She was terribly upset until Mother quoted a very appropriate Russian proverb which translates as:

"You don't weep over loss of hair of the beheaded, do you? Two people are dependent on your support if they are to make it. What is education, or anything for that matter, in that context? Nothing. Life is more important than any achievement we may meet. It is nothing if we pay for it with someone else's life."

My sister got the message and never again raised the subject. For a while she was a bit subdued, but then compassion took over. With her there, my brother and I did not spend quite as long on our own. Lucya used to come after milking, with our fresh supply of milk, and sometimes during the day as well. My sister was very good to us. I felt secure in the knowledge that Mum and Lucya would take care of us no matter what came along.

The bonding between my Malchick and I was so close he shifted more and more of his mother bonding to me. He could not bear to let me out of his sight. If anyone raised their voice in our presence, he would quickly look at me to see if I was affected by it. If he thought I was, he would burst into tears. He became my shield. To this day I feel a great affinity for all the little ones and am an outright magnet to two-year-olds. I am sure it is connected to that experience, particularly in view of the fact that he died of malnutrition only half a year or so later. He never got much beyond two and I never really got over it.

Fifty years later I weep as I write. I was not as aware of all this when I was young and had children of my own who lived, but now that they've all grown up and have families of their own, I miss them and remember and relive this part of my childhood, the unresolved grief and pain in particular. I think that writing it down helps to put it to rest and to heal.

We spent spring and most of the summer in this beautiful village. Once the warm weather arrived, we were all filled with the joy of simply being alive, not hungry and cold, and Mum not having to go out into the night for *buryan*. We saw a lot more of Mum and my sister and had all the food we needed to keep us healthy.

However, the German front began to deteriorate and once again we knew we had to move, and to run again from the communists. Firstly, we went to the town where my Aunt Lydia and her children and my other sister, Irma, were and together we began our very slow journey to Crimea. It all depended on the strength or the weakness of the front. When it was strong, we moved, but when it did not do so well, we stopped completely. For most of our journey we heard the fighting and at night it lit up the sky, like fireworks, except it was not. People were being killed and maimed. As we heard and saw the tragedy of war before our eyes.

Our stepfather joined us in Caucasus. I think he had also deserted, so we had two men to help us move. We stayed in a village for some months, this time a Russian/German one. Its occupants had been sent to Siberia a year earlier and it really looked like a German village, with neat streets and two-storey houses all painted white. Having been abandoned for a year, though, it truly was a ghost town. The growing conditions there were ideal, with good soil, lots of rain and a very mild climate. Consequently, the vegetation was thick and tall; even reaching to the tops of houses. Sometimes it was a bit frightening moving through all that growth and not knowing what we were going to meet or step on.

However, the bigger fear was of the front.

Crops had been left in the fields, so there was corn, sunflowers, wheat and other grains, all left to themselves for a year. A lot of it had self-sown, especially the grain. We would not have gone hungry if we had had the means to grind the wheat and the facilities for cooking, but we had neither. Adults soaked and chewed wheat, but it was not that simple for the little ones. Their mothers would chew the wheat for them and then put it in their children's mouths, but it was not enough. The children looked hungry and were losing good condition, much to their mothers' horror.

As if that was not enough, we had a mouse plague. The rodents just took over as there was plenty for them to eat. The floor of any house had a living grey carpet, a carpet of mice. We could not just walk on them, as they would jump and bite. So, we shuffled our feet, minimising the number we stepped on. They squealed when they were trodden on. We could not leave the house as outside it was just as bad. We could not leave anyone unprotected from the mice, as they would just demolish anything that kept still. We slept on table tops whenever possible, shooing the mice off ourselves and each other. No one did much sleeping. Mind you, they were not as active in the dark.

Our little boy was getting thinner and weaker. All our efforts were not enough. He got pneumonia. Mum sat up with him night after night, protecting him from the mice. Our Malchick was getting towards the end of his life. Mum would not leave him for a moment, constantly holding him. His beautiful blue eyes stayed closed. We all knew he would not last long, and our biggest fear was Mum going with him. She, too, was terribly thin and could hardly walk.

One morning she woke up, sitting up with her hands on Malchick and screaming "No, Mum! No, Mum!" She had dreamed that her dead mother had come into the room, wearing a big black shawl around her shoulders, walking up to Malchick, picking him up and putting him inside the shawl and disappearing. Our Malchick died that same day. No one could shift Mother from the cot he was in.

I have not said much about Malchick's father, my stepfather. He expressed his pain and grief in silence. No one heard him utter a word for days before Malchick died. On hearing of his death, he just walked away into the distance. Mother sat with Malchick all day. At dusk, my stepfather returned. He just looked at Mum and did not say a word. Mum picked Malchick up, wrapped him securely – I remember her checking his feet to make sure they were tucked in and covered, and then she followed my stepfather out of the house.

They walked up a hill, where my stepfather had planted a birch tree on the top of the hill. On reaching the location, they both stopped before a little grave my stepfather had dug earlier. What frightened me the most was that neither spoke, wept or screamed. There was just this unbearable silence. Slowly, Mum kneeled on the ground holding my little brother tight to her chest with my stepfather holding a shovel. It all seemed to take place in slow motion, as if there was a remote-control at work. Finally, she placed Malchick in the little pit, which was not very deep. Our brother just lay there with his eyes closed. Mum pulled his robe over his face and his father covered him gently with such care that it seemed as though he was lifting granite instead of soil. On finishing the task, he pressed down the soil with his big hands as if he was making sure Malchick was comfortable.

In the meantime, it had got quite dark. I whispered to Mum to come with me to the others, but she did not seem to hear me, and I remembered the other time she did not seem to hear me when Father was taken. I became very frightened. Maybe it was not possible to return a second time from wherever she went to. I was also grieving for the loss of Malchick, yet I had no one to comfort me or share the pain with. My mother and stepfather seemed to have turned into stone. I really panicked at the thought of losing Mum at the same time as Malchick, who was an extension of myself, a part of me on this little hill with a birch tree.

We somehow continued on with both the mouse plague and the

fighting front. Mum just sat there, staring into space and seemingly seeing nothing.

I felt like saying to Mum, "I am hurting, too. He was part of me. Please let us grieve together." I said nothing, though. I was sure that if I had, she would not have heard. The isolation, the solo journey through grief was hard to bear. I desperately needed someone with me, someone to hold me and say, "We will make it."

Ever so slowly we returned to Crimea. I was sure we had lost Mum. She just sat in silence.

What finally brought Mum around was a Jewish family, whose lives she had saved when in Caucasus when all the other Jews had been executed. This family had kept within close range of my mother. The strain on them must have been extraordinary: to have seen people of their ethnoreligious group executed while they were still alive. They were trying to save their son, who was about seven or eight. If they hadn't had any children, I am sure they would have preferred to die with their people. Garbachowski was the family's name and the father had been our butcher before the war. Actually, only he was Jewish, as his wife was German, like us.

The Russians were going to intern them because of the German wife and then they nearly lost their lives because he was Jewish – how ironic life can be. It must have been close to 1942 when rumours started to circulate about the execution of the Jews in Russia. Mrs Garbachowski came to our village to see Mum and told her of the rumours.

"Rumours are getting stronger and stronger," she said. "There must be truth in them, what shall I do?"

Mum replied, "Go to the head SS man of the district and don't leave until you find the gentle side of him. We all have a conscience, and even inside that formidable uniform is a human being. He is someone's son, someone's husband, someone's father, too. Now it is up to you to find that part of him. Go to him, tell him the truth and don't leave until he finds a way for you to escape execution."

The ball ended up in Mum's court pretty quickly. Mrs Garbachowski came back in a few days to say that she did find a very receptive person inside that uniform, but he could only help her if she found someone who would state formally that they were both German. There was one other stipulation: if her husband looked like her, there was no chance of saving them. She had beautiful black hair, waist long, and a dark complexion and, for all of the world, looked very Jewish. He added she'd better guard her passport with her life because, without it, she would be taken for a Jew. But she had no concerns there, as her husband's looks were the opposite to hers. He was blond with blue eyes, for all the world a German.

The head of the district would not take her word for it, so he created a scenario to help them achieve their objective. The plan was this: first Mum had to go to town and meet the SS man to guarantee that Mr Garbachowski was German and that on registration day they would depart in whichever direction he pointed. If he could not help them, he would point to the Jewish queue but, if he could help, he would point to the German queue.

Mum went to see the SS man. He pointed out the risk she was taking by harbouring a Jew and putting her own life on the line.

She answered, "I know".

"And you still want to do it?" he asked.

"Yes," she replied.

Soon after this we were all called to be registered. First there was a queue which included many races, and later it split into three: Russian, German and Jew. When we reached the point of separation of races, the plan was that this SS man would come out of his office and indicate which way they were to go. I remember clearly how we stopped at that point and no one came out to indicate. It seemed a very long time before we saw him come out and another eternity before the signal came.

Poor Mrs Garbachowski was being supported by Mum on one side, her husband on the other. The tension was horrific but, at last, the officer pointed to the German queue. She had to be held up by us all as her legs just folded under her. On seeing the signal, we registered, and the Garbachowskis were safe.

I watched all the Jewish people in their queue and wondered what awaited them. Maybe the bad things we had heard about were all just rumours. They looked so dejected and sad and I could not get them out of my mind, but we had to move on. There seemed no point to it all. No one appeared to know what was happening let alone why. One word was supposed to answer it all: '*war*'.

We went back to our village. Mum had to go back to the kindergarten and Lucya, too, as they worked together.

How do you describe something so hugely appalling? There are no words for it. The Garbachowski family fitted into that category. They stayed in the town of our registration and had to behave in a regular fashion. They watched the rest of the Jewish people isolated in barracks, surrounded by a barbed wire fence and guarded by armed men. Their isolation must have indicated to them that they were in danger.

A week or so later, the waiting was over. Where the Jewish people had been there was just a pile of clothing in the middle of the yard. Before that, when my aunty went to work, she had to go past the yard and the barracks – she hated going past and seeing the inmates' empty eyes staring into nothingness. Once she got nearer the fence she almost ran. The terrible feelings she got almost overwhelmed her.

Then, one morning, there were no more people, just the pile of clothing. That morning she ran back home and wept bitterly as she told her husband the story. He calmed her down and told her she had to go to work and act as if she had seen nothing or we would all be in danger if we showed our disapproval. Besides, we didn't know what had happened to those people. My middle sister, Irma, too, had seen the empty yard and the pile of clothing when she came to our village to visit Mum. Once again, she had been confronted by a wolf sitting in the middle of the road, but this time she had no fear.

"I have to reach Mum. I have to reach Mum," she kept saying to herself, with tears streaming down her face. The wolf, on seeing this fast-moving something coming straight at itself, just ran away.

By the time she reached us, her face was pitch black with baked-on earth mixed with tears. Mum got a terrible shock, but calmed Irma down, washed her face and gave her something to.

"Just drink this milk," Mum said. "Tell me what has upset you?"

"Mum, where are all those people?" Irma replied. "What happened to them?"

"Maybe they got shifted to another camp," Mum said.

"But Mum, what about their clothes?"

"I don't know," was all Mum could say. Each of us was left with our own thoughts. We did not have an answer, but each felt terrible chills going down our spines.

As I remember it

We did not have to wait long to find out what had happened. A young man, whom we knew from somewhere during our travels, arrived on our doorstep so distressed he could not speak at first. Mum calmed him down, to the point where he began to pour out the cause of his distress, and 'pour out' was the only way to describe it. It tumbled out of him incoherently as if having he was a nightmare. Finally, Mum picked up enough pieces to understand the reason for his distress, he told her what had given him such a shock and had nearly cost him his sanity, perhaps already had.

The story went as follows: he was going through a forest one day and stumbled on a freshly dug enormous hole. Apparently 20 people could stand side by side to fill the space, which they later did. Before he had a chance to disappear, he heard lots of voices in the distance. He hid, but he could still see the massive hole and could not get away from there without being seen, so he lay still and watched. A large group of people came into view with guards all around them. He could not tell us how many people there were, but it was a lot. On reaching the site, people were told to line up at the edge of the hole. A firing squad was on the opposite side. An order was given: "Fire!".

The people fell into the hole face down. This was repeated until no more people were left. He said most of them died with dignity, but some pleaded for mercy. One girl, in particular, made it almost impossible for one executor to pull the trigger. Almost, as she still fell to the rifles. Apparently, she was exceptionally beautiful. She stared hypnotically into an executioner's eyes and held them. He could not pull his trigger and all fell into the hole except her. The officer screamed his orders, but still the gunman could not do it, until a gun was pointed at his own head. He then closed his eyes and pulled the trigger. When he opened them, the young woman was down with the others and a new lot of people was lined up.

The young man who witnessed all this waited for the army to return to its station before he could move and make his way to our village and Mum. We could not even establish when all this happened. His hair had turned white and he lost hold of his life completely. We never found out his fate, he just moved on as if in a dream from which he would never wake. If only it had been a dream. He carried with him a particularly horrendous nightmare.

How is it possible for such evil to be carried out by humans on other humans? Yes, you could have an earthquake that swallowed up just as many people, but this was different. It was carried out by one human being against another. Just cold-blooded killing. My conclusion is that Satan does enter people and we must never forget it.

Soon after that, the front started to deteriorate further, and we began our journey back to Crimea with the Garbachowski family always within easy reach of Mum, who was still grieving after Malchick's death. They were just as concerned about Mum as we were. She was their only link with life, but little by little she found her way back to life: their pleading faces reached her and led her to themselves and to us.

My stepfather was a different story, as he just got stuck in his grief. We watched him moving further and further away from life and I recalled him saying to Malchick as he buried him, "I won't be long." It was very sad to see a man of his size and intelligence just waste away. This was the second time in his life that he had lost family to starvation, and both times it could have been prevented.

To Mother, he just said, "I am so sorry, darling."

My mother was in a state of trauma all the way to Crimea. The Garbachowskis were always around, however, and that comforted me because I knew Mum would not let them down, as she was all they had. Three people's lives were in her hands. I am sure there was a superhuman strength that made Mum return, but to what degree she healed no one knows. She made no reference to our little brother nor his death for years.

My stepfather just got weaker day by day and he was eventually admitted to hospital. The doctors called my mother asking her what could be wrong with him, as they could not find any physiological symptoms at all. The doctors were puzzled and my mother didn't enlighten them about our loss and grief.

It was many years later, when I was an adult, that she spoke for the first time about our little brother and his death, but even then, you could not touch on the subject or elaborate beyond the point she was prepared to go.

Malchick's father died of unknown causes. To my mother, he just said, "I am sorry, darling. Not even for you can I make myself go on. I want to go to my son."

The Garbachowskis became my mother's lifeline as much as she was theirs. One night Mrs Garbachowski ran to our house in hysterics. Mum ran back with her to find that her husband had hung himself. The two women cut him down and revived him and Mother stayed with them for the rest of the night. She asked him what had brought this on and got to the bottom of it. Apparently, a man they both knew from before the war made a comment to Mr Garbachowski, referring to him being Jewish. Mother was appalled. She comforted them both and assured them that they would not have any problem with this man again after she had spoken to him. She also pointed out to Mr Garbachowski that if he killed himself, it would be investigated and their true identity revealed, and that his wife and herself would be executed the next day.

She paid a visit to the man who had made the comment. To my knowledge, Mum had never threatened anyone before or done so since, but on this day she did. She told this man to do his best to make sure Mr Garbachowski lived, because if he was identified and executed, the same fate would befall him as she would go to the authorities and report him as a Russian spy. This man's wife came to see my mother three days later asking her what she had said to him as he had not left his room for three days. He had taken it seriously all right and he began to protect Mr Garbachowski. People took notice of him as he had known Mr Garbachowski since before the war and the news that he was not Jewish, but German, began to circulate. Of course, there was always the risk of bumping into someone else who knew this man as the town he came from was only a couple of miles away. The chances of him being recognised were great as he used to be the town's butcher.

Mr Garbachowski was all right, and he and his wife and son made it. We left Russia together, but later lost track of them. I often think of them and wonder how on earth they managed to keep their sanity after seeing much of their race destroyed while escaping the same fate and surrounded by authorities responsible for the atrocities. I would love to be able to trace their son as the parents are most likely dead. I registered with the Red Cross, but they have not been able to locate him.

In 1943 my family, my aunty and her family and the Garbachowskis set out once again on our journey to escape the evil of Russian communism.

However, we had spent a whole year in Crimea before being on the run again. I search my mind for happy memories of that time, but find very few. Our grief for our little brother was still very fresh. Somehow, he seemed to tie us, the big ones, together, minimising our past traumas and having us focus on love, which was what we needed the most. Now he was gone, and the front was raging where he was buried in his shallow grave, we hoped the birch tree would survive the attacks. If we could have gone back to where he was buried, it would have helped us to heal, of this, I am sure. As it was, we left him all alone on a little hill with a birch tree, which was just as vulnerable as his little grave. There was no opportunity to heal.

Once again life became very serious indeed. We had to leave our country. The alternative was death, yet it was still a horrendous step into the unknown.

Chapter 4 – 1943, leaving Russia

In 1943[7] we found ourselves on the run again, running for our lives from communism. The Germans also began their retreat. As slow as it was, we wanted to be out of reach of the evil of communism, which was like a malignant cancer that no one could stop. For a while it had seemed that the occupation of Russia by the Germans would save Russia from the clutches of communism. The Russian people had welcomed the occupying forces, not because they knew anything about the German ideology, but purely because, since the revolution, there had not been an opportunity to stand up to the evil of Russian communism. The power of the communists was built on purges, labour camps in Siberia, executions and starvation. Whole towns were wiped out and there was no help from the West, even though foreign reporters filmed frozen corpses in the streets.

As the front deteriorated and the Germans began their retreat from Russia, we tried to keep ahead of the retreat so as not to get caught in the net of communism. We had lived in the Crimea for almost a year, not very far from our home town, which we could walk to.

My sister Irma, who was 13 at the time, begged my mother to go to our town and present ourselves to the man who was responsible for our father's arrest and disappearance to make him pay for the terrible thing he had done.

---

[7] In early 1943, the Germans began to withdraw and consolidate their positions in the region due to setbacks elsewhere. They established a defensive line in the Taman Peninsula, from which they hoped to eventually launch new operations in the Caucasus. The fighting remained reasonably static until September 1943 when the Germans ordered fresh withdrawals, which effectively ended the period of fighting in the Caucasus.

My mother refused, though, and said, "It will not bring Father back, and besides, the vengeance-seeker always gets committed to crime, so no, I will not be part of that. If he gets shot for his crime, and he should have been, how would that make you feel better? It will make you feel worse, of this, I am sure!"

"But, Mum, at least let us present ourselves to him in silence," Irma replied. "He saw us as we were before he betrayed Father, so let him look at us and see what effect he had on four other people as well as Father. Please, Mum, please!"

"It will cause us more pain than anything else," Mum said. "Leave it to God. This man will have enough trouble both living and dying with his conscience. We don't need to add to it."

Mum did, however, walk alone to the town from which we had been torn a year earlier at the commencement of the World War II in Russia in 1941. She did not want us to get upset at seeing the destruction of our home. She was hoping to find some of our personal things that were of no use to other people. She returned empty handed. Not a single item could she find. It was only a year after we had had to go, leaving everything behind, and I mean *everything* – photographs, knick-knacks, etc, no trace of anything. It had all disappeared.

My mother frequently used a proverb which translates well into English and made a lot of sense:

"You don't weep over loss of hair of the beheaded. We have life, we must not grieve over the loss of possessions. There is enough to weep over for the loss of loved ones. Material things one can always acquire, providing one has life."

So, here we were, a year later, and once again on the move. We wanted to get as far as possible from communism.

Mother had twice experienced the enforced *Galadovka* starvation. The first time was when she was still married to her first husband and all grain had been removed from the town, with just enough left for the law enforcers to survive. Then the Siberian winter arrived, and people froze to death wherever they happened to be positioned. The reason she had survived was because her husband was a doctor and there was a great shortage of professional people. Spring was a second nightmare. As the corpses thawed, typhoid spread, for there was no one to bury the dead. Until they died, people had flocked to the doctor's door, and this is why so many froze at Mum's doorstep.

The second time was in 1931 or '32, when I was a baby. My mother had been widowed by then, and she later married my father who was a high school teacher. She often talked about the *Galadovka* starvation. My eldest sister Lucya, who was six, remembered it well. Mother was 27 at that time and father 25. Father was very athletic, fit and strong; Mother was breastfeeding me and yet, it was Father who started to swell from hunger first, not Mum. She used to worry about him lasting the distance and he would worry about her and the baby. Every morsel he could find he would try to feed to Mum.

Mum kept saying to him, "Peter, you are underestimating nature. I am the producer of life, so nature will make sure that I live."

And she was right, as Father would have died a long time before her.

The threat of yet another *Galadovka* was one of many, many reasons for us leaving Russia, but our list of reasons for going seemed endless. Yes, we wanted to remove ourselves as far as possible from the Kremlin. Aleksandr Solzhenitsyn tells us that more than 60 million people fell to the axe of Russian communism. Yes, we had very, very good reasons for leaving Russia.

Because it is a peninsula, leaving the Crimea was not easy. The Russians knew that anyone who could leave would do so. Consequently, they bombed the little strips of land that joined it to the Ukraine, so no one could leave through there. The only option left was to cross the Black Sea, but this, too, was bombed. Being such a large area, however, the shelling was not as effective. It gave us a chance to escape.

It is all part of the reason why we sat on the wharf of Yevpatoriya on the Black Sea trying to run to freedom, risking our lives rather than staying and continuing in the cruel system of the Kremlin. As we sat there, ships came and went, but there was no room for us. They were all busy fighting a war and killing each other, no room for people seeking freedom.

Then, one beautiful morning, another ship arrived. People rushed forward and soon it was full and we missed out once again.

"Never mind," Mum said. "There will be others, so don't worry."

By dusk, a barge had arrived with a handful of survivors from the ship that had left that same morning. One family is still vividly in my mind. The father and three teenage children had jumped from the sinking ship onto the barge. The mother had jumped as the ship jerked further down and she had landed between the barge and the ship and drowned. One boy had an eye missing. It was so tragic and sad.

The captain of the barge looked at us and said, "This is not much of a recommendation," pointing at the few survivors of the morning ship. "If you wish to try your luck you are very welcome. I have space for you, and I will be leaving at last light."

Mum thanked him and just sat very still as if waiting for an answer to come from somewhere, then quietly said, "We will board. Sitting here will lead to certain death. In trying to cross there is a chance we will survive."

So, we boarded. We sat on the supplies. The captain told us our heads were too close to the top of the barge as they had anti-aircraft guns on the top deck, so we slid down. It was a strange evening, so unreal it was almost mystical.

People present all felt we would never make it, which put them in a mood you don't see any other time in life.

The evening seemed endless. People were rushing backwards and forwards with such determination it was as if their lives depended on it. Then a sense of excitement filled the air. People knew they were likely to die, and yet the atmosphere was that of exhilaration, almost carnival-like. Strands of music drifted to our ears. It was coming from the sailors' quarters and it was getting louder and louder as people became intoxicated. Desperate people were doing desperate things. As I looked around, I realised that we were the only ones still sitting on our bundles, as everyone else was at the 'party'. I can still see the captain's handsome face as he invited my mother to join them.

Mother looked him straight in the eye and said, "It all depends on what you are inviting me for."

He looked a bit embarrassed as he said, "A cup of tea or something."

"Thank you, sir, but it is not my cup of tea, and the 'something' is another problem!"

I can still see his blushing face as he took off his cap, gave a little bow and moved on without another word. Their conversation puzzled me at the time, and it disappointed me not to be part of the fun. I decided my mother was strange and no one loved her as they loved the other girls' mothers. I could see how they and their mothers were showered with gifts. I did not want the gifts, but I felt so sorry for my mother, to always be alone. The reason she did not participate in that kind of activity only became clear to me when I was an adult myself.

The partying went on right through the night. Desperate people grabbing a bit of life and numbing themselves with alcohol, for in a matter of hours they expected to die.

As dawn broke, the realisation that a moment of truth was at hand hit everyone. With the light, bombers would attempt to sink us.

An eerie silence fell upon the little barge. I walked to a railing, looked around and realised we were part of a large convoy. One of the ships was enormous and had big red crosses all over it. No one could miss this as being a ship full of wounded people, but Russia had no sympathy for the injured and maimed. They would sink that ship just like any other target. We all knew that. I remember thinking of all the wounded and suffering going down. Somehow it seemed a lot worse for them than for us.

I was mesmerised by the beauty and the size of the ship and, as I watched it, noticed something moving towards us. On the water It looked like a toy boat. I pointed it out to someone and was instantly thrown face-down. It was a torpedo, but somehow our little barge had dodged it.

A silence prevailed and I wanted to scream just to break it, but couldn't. I opened my mouth, but no sound came out. The silence continued. We heard distant splashes as aircraft dropped their bombs. I stood and stared at the ship with the red cross on it, saying to myself, "This won't happen, this won't happen. Not this beautiful ship with hurting people."

The planes came closer to us, and the splashes. Some targets were hit, some missed. I rejoiced at the thought that they might miss us altogether. Finally, we heard the sound of the planes' engines leaving as they flew back to reload. This was little comfort to us, though, as we realised that they knew our position. It wouldn't take long for them to reload and return to complete their mission.

My clearest memory is of the silence, which continued. Only the sailors moved about and did their duty, but they also seemed to be working in silence.

"Have I gone deaf?" I wondered. But then I could hear the splash of the sea so I concluded I couldn't be deaf.

Once again, we heard the familiar sound of straining engines. This time they seemed even heavier and slower, but heading towards us all the same. They were getting closer and closer and, finally, they were overhead and the big splashes were *really* close. Water went high into the air as they dropped their bombs.

Suddenly, it all stopped. Even the anti-aircraft guns stopped. We could hear the planes – they were so low, yet we could not see them. We heard bombs dropping but missing targets. Eventually, I ventured to the rail of the barge. It seemed so bizarre. What had stopped the planes from hitting their targets?

As I strained my eyes, trying in vain to see, it struck me that we seemed to be either inside a cloud or under the sea. The cloud was so low and dense and the rain so fine that it really did seem as though we were under water and invisible to the planes, which dropped all their bombs haphazardly and flew back to their home base. The clouds followed us all the way to Odessa, our destination.

This occurrence is still a mystery. I cherish the memory of this experience because I owe my life to it. It was inexplicable. Our convoy stayed intact.

On arrival to the other side of the Black Sea we were all so stunned by the experience of our escape that it seemed we were in some kind of dream or trance and would wake up any moment to find ourselves drowning, sinking to the bottom of the sea.

On disembarking, Mother spread our few belongings on the grass to dry. As she did so, a woman came towards us, hesitating before approaching us. She looked strange, but then, all of humanity looked strange in war time. Mother asked her if she had lost one of her family members.

She said: "No, I have found what I was looking for. I wanted to find the person for whom God saved our barge, in fact, the whole convoy. And when I saw you, I knew it was you."

Mother stopped what she was doing, looked at the woman and smiled as she said, "I am no different from you or anyone else. It was for the good in all of us that He saved the convoy."

The woman persisted though. "You were the only one on our barge who wasn't at the party last night," she said. "You were with your children. I didn't mean to embarrass you, I just wanted you to know what an impact all this had on me and somehow you are in the centre of it." Then she walked away to her bundle and children.

Another picture clearly imprinted in my mind is that of a tall, barbed wire fence with hungry men behind it. It frightened me and then I heard them speak in Russian. We stared at them in shock.

"Please, please, don't throw that bread away. Give it to us." they pleaded.

Mum walked towards the fence and said, "But this bread is soaked in sea water, you can't eat that."

Their calls became more urgent. We walked over to the barbed wire fence and, with outstretched arms, they grabbed the bread and ate it as only the famished can. They were Russian prisoners of war whom Stalin did not recognise: he called them traitors. They were the forgotten people. The Red Cross had no access to them, and they were starving. We held their hands through the fence and spoke only briefly as we heard a cattle train in the distance. The year was 1943, and we doubted they would survive the war.

Everything was moving so fast. There was no time to pause, no time to think, just this enormous mountain of feelings, of pain and suffering everywhere we looked. The woman who approached us, the prisoners of war, their eyes so big, standing out all the more in their hollow faces as their bodies had no weight on them.

In the distance, the rumbling noise of a train reached our ears. We looked at the prisoners of war pressing themselves against the barbed wire as if trying to push it down to follow us. We girls burst into tears, but Mum just kept moving towards our bundles. We saw the train approaching in the distance, then picked our bundles up while looking back at the prisoners as we boarded the train.

We had no food and or idea of when we would be able to obtain some. We were past feeling hungry: it was like when you fast, that same kind of lightheadedness. Still, we had life and hope and hung on to those.

In war zones one seemed always to be in a hurry, a bit like fast-forwarding a film. The carriages were mostly packed to standing room. Children slumped at their mothers' feet, while their mothers stood, legs astride, to protect their children. People pushed each other, as if they could create more space by doing this. Mothers were shouting, "You are standing on my child!" and so on.

My mother managed to get a corner spot, away from the opening. She told me to sit down in the corner while she protected me by standing over me. It was really scary being on the train floor with the crush of humanity hovering overhead, pushing each other. I felt as though they were all going to land on top of me at any moment, yet, I had complete trust in my mother. When she said that it would be all right, then I knew it would be. I just closed my eyes, blocked my ears and somehow went to sleep to the rhythm of the moving train.

We were on our way to be 'cleaned', as the Germans called it, and deloused. It always amazed me how little time it took for lice to find us once we were on the road without any means of keeping clean. They quickly grew to become large and fat, and you could pick one out of your hair and squash it with your nails! This would produce a cracking noise or a little bang. It was terrible being invaded by parasites. People's heads that were too infested by lice were shaved – it looked terrible, and it was cold without hair to keep one warm.

We arrived in Poland, disembarked and were taken to a camp. Next, we went to a large hall to be inspected. We had to shed all our clothes and walk into the hall naked. The soldiers on guard made us feel embarrassed at first, but later we became indifferent. As we were being moved it seemed as if we were one unit, not individuals. It was just-wall to-wall naked people. Mind you, we were mainly women and children, so that made it a little more tolerable. At the other end we received our deloused, sterilised clothing after we had had a good scrub. It was wonderful to feel clean again and wear clean clothes.

We did not stay long in Poland for we were soon taken to a camp in Austria. That, too, was clean and there was food in abundance. What a joy this was for people who came from a country of shortages and starvation.

It was 1943. I was 12, but looked more like a nine-year-old. I was put into hospital to build up my strength. All I really needed was food, but it had to be administered by a doctor. I was checked thoroughly and weighed regularly. It was wonderful getting all this attention and having no more hunger pangs.

It was there that I met a man who had been in the same prison as my father after he had been taken from us by the NKVD. We had heard not a single word of his fate for six years and here was a man who had spent considerable time with him. We were ecstatic.

The man was a quadriplegic as a result of his prison experience, which had included much torture. He could not move a single muscle from the head down. It was a strange sight: he looked so big and strong, yet was pinned down to immobility. He had a wonderful mind and spirit, however, and his heart was full of love. He told us that he had been in the same prison as Dad for three years, until the winds of war began to blow. He recognised my father in me, as, apparently, I looked very much like him.

I ran to get my mother and tell her that there was a man in the hospital that had known Dad after he'd been taken from us. I wanted to run, until I looked at my mother, who seemed to be having difficulty walking. She moved so slowly, and I did not understand until much later that she had almost frozen into immobility. She made her way to the ward where this man lay ever so slowly.

I wanted to say, "Mum, this man touched our dad and spoke to him, and spent lots and lots of time with him," but one look at Mum stopped me.

Finally, we stood before him. I just wanted to be near the man who had been so close to my father in the intimacy of a prison setting. They had been hurt together, and had comforted each other, even though there was no room for hope as they all knew their fate. I had so many questions to ask. What did Dad say to him about us? Did he mention me? Yet, standing there and listening to this man's conversation with Mum, I realised the pain they were experiencing was so great that I could not utter a word in case I added more to it.

Mother spent quite a lot of time with this man until we had to move on. He told us that Father took the blow of losing us very hard and his unknown fate was made harder because he knew that Mother would never betray him. He also knew the price for that.

His fellow prisoners would try to pull him out of his despair by saying, "Look here, Peter, we, too, have left families behind, yet somehow we need to find something to hold on to or we will go insane. Come, let us draw strength from each other."

The thing that used to distress Dad the most was his knowledge that he would *never* see a report in the paper in which Mother denounced him, agreeing publicly with the authorities that he was, indeed, a criminal, an enemy of the people, and have their marriage annulled. When he said this to his fellow prisoners, they brushed it aside as him idealising his wife, making a saint out of her.

"You will see, it will appear in the paper," they said. "No woman will let her children die if she can prevent it."

He just shook his head in despair and said, "No, I will never see that in the paper."

He also knew the penalty for defying the NKVD. He imagined her interrogations, her suffering, compounded by not knowing if she had escaped the Soviet Union or if she had been killed or if the children had been put in an orphanage. He never did know our fate. All he knew was that she did not give in to them as the *Pravda* paper was never given to him with a published declaration of her rejection of him.

It was so wonderful to be with this man who had been with Father for three years. Because of the man's quadriplegic state, his wife had managed to have him released so that she could take care of him. At that time, the prisons of Crimea were full of people like my father:

not actual criminals. The war with Germany put them at even greater risk as most political prisoners were genetically German. In fact, once the war began, the people not moved to Siberia were just blown up. Whole prisons were destroyed, and everyone wiped out.

We have never been able to find out what father's fate was. According to this man, he lived for three years after being imprisoned and that was all we knew.

We did hear from someone who knew Father well that he saw a whole lot of prisoners marching through the streets. I presume the guards were shifting them from one prison to another. The reason this other man recognised Father was because he was the only one who was looking around, stumbling and falling. They were dressed in the usual striped prison garb and barefoot, and Father kept looking around in the hope of seeing one of us. This image used to haunt me a lot, the impression of a very thin young man in striped attire looking around, but not able to separate himself from the rest of the inmates. They were all chained together, falling, being pulled up by the persons on either side, shouted at by guards. The bare feet, cold ground and this man looking around is such a vivid picture in my mind.

I remember thinking: if only we could have got a glimpse of him, just a passing glimpse would have been better than never to see him again. We had had no time to say goodbye, no last special words. He never did get a chance to buy me a doll. I wanted to tell him that it was all right, it was him and only him that I ever wanted, not the things he provided for us. There was no opportunity to finalise anything.

Along with our quadriplegic friend, my mother was approached to write an autobiography. They both chose not to, as it was too painful, but also because, as Mother said, we didn't know yet who was going to win the war. What if the Russians did? We would have been the first to be executed. This was 1943, and hopes were still pinned on Germany ridding Russia of communism. This wise man was not going to risk all for a moment of glory. His and Mother's stories were certainly worth recording, but it was not worth risking their lives and the lives of others.

Chapter 5 – Yugoslavia

We did not stay very long in that camp in Austria as, with the men away fighting, workforces were needed everywhere. Mother volunteered to go wherever she was most needed. That turned out to be on the land. The farmers were just not coping because of a shortage of workers, so, away we went, all the way to Slovenia, in northern Yugoslavia.

By that time a girl from an orphanage in Crimea had 'adopted' our family, so there we were, one delicate, cultured-looking lady and four teenagers who were going to become farm workers. It was not a surprise that at the end of the day, at the place where farmers came for their labourers, we were the only ones who had not been offered jobs. The yard where everyone gathered was large, so we felt quite conspicuous, just sitting there with nowhere to go and no one wanting us. As we pondered our fate, we saw a tall, handsome man slowly, but confidently, walking towards us. He was wearing a big hat and could only be a farmer.

On approaching us he smiled and said, "Are you part of the workforce?"

My mother stood up to all of her 5' 2" of height, looked him straight in the eye and said, "Don't judge a book by its cover, sir."

"You have courage as well, to stand up to me when I am your only hope in escaping the partisans," he replied.

Mum said, "Again, don't judge us as being useless without giving us a chance to prove our worth."

"Well, well, I certainly cannot leave you here to be raped or killed by the partisans," he said. "Hop on my wagon. I will take you home with me, but only until the morning when I will bring you back, because I really need farm workers."

The man's widowed mother saw us coming and nearly had a fit while she yelled, "Johan, I knew you were a bit daft, but I did not know you were completely stupid! Did I send you out to pick up refugees or workers?"

He apologised for his mother and said, "She is not really as bad as she sounds, please forgive her."

He then led us to an empty house, a beautiful A-shaped pine construction. It soon became dark, and no lights were allowed. Johan came back with some food for us. We thanked him and really, really enjoyed whatever it was. We hadn't eaten all day, so we were very hungry. I went to sleep with his kind face before my eyes. I had a strong feeling that we were going to be happy here, even if it was only for a little while.

The sound of milking woke me up long before dawn. Milk hitting a metal bucket makes quite a loud noise and the rhythm of the milking brought back wonderful memories from when I was five and my mother used to milk our cow, then the sound of the milk being poured into glasses. So, I woke to the joy of a familiar sound then stretched out my hand to where Mum should be, but she was not there. I was sure that she must have been one of the milkers.

I found out later that Mum, too, had heard the sound of milking in the dark and had gone to the barn to help. There were about 10 or so cows to be milked, which was quite a job for one person, so Mum's help was very much appreciated. Nevertheless, the woman, the farm owner, said to Mum that we had to leave after breakfast because she needed workers.

Mum just said, "This will contribute sufficiently towards our breakfast. We are not beggars."

The woman did not reply.

After breakfast, when it was time for the kind man to take us back through the forest to the labour yard, it began to rain, so we waited for it to stop but, instead, it turned into a deluge. Mother noticed a basketful of mending next to a sewing machine, so she found the owner and offered to do some sewing.

"All right," she grumbled.

The rain kept up, not only all morning, but also through the afternoon and until evening came. No one ventured outside. By the end of the day the basket was almost empty, and Mother had won the owner's respect.

"Hmmm," she mumbled. "You are not just a pretty city person. You may even be useful in the fields. You can stay even though you have other mouths to feed."

This is how we came to spend four seasons in rural Yugoslavia. We proved the owner wrong on all counts. We had come from Russia where life was so hard to hang on to and survival a daily challenge. Compared to that, working on a farm and being well fed was paradise.

My sisters, myself and the orphan girl who had adopted us made four mouths for one worker to feed. In the mornings we went to school and worked in the fields in the afternoons. Mum was multi-skilled and working full-time on the farm came to a lot more than just our keep. We were not paid wages for our efforts, as this was war, and all had to work for nothing more than their keep and to 'help the war effort'. I am sure that every country at war used the same slogan.

As I remember it

Our stay began early in summer when everything was growing. The fields were all beautifully green and sunflowers reached up to the heavens as they stretched for the sun. There was an abundance of stone fruit and cherries, which we had never known in Russia – there was never plenty of any food there. We children concluded that this was paradise!

While working in the fields we always got a special treat. In the heat of the day a big barrel of apple cider would be brought, just when we were at our thirstiest. Everyone got so happy on it that I later wondered if it was alcoholic. Well, whatever it was, it made the workers happy, and they would work off the alcohol with their labour.

By then, other farmers had heard of this Russian family who could do anything, worked really hard and sang beautiful songs in the evenings. Offers came in thick and fast to entice us to work on their farms for far greater rewards. Mum just smiled and thanked them for their offers, but declined.

She would simply say, "This farm took us in when we were desperate, and it would not be right for us to go to a higher bidder."

Yes, we did love singing. Mum accompanied us on a guitar. With no lights allowed there was little else we could do, so our singing improved considerably during those months. I have very happy memories of the time we spent there. I could not get over the fact that one could eat when hungry and eat the food of choice! This was foreign to all who came from Russia, other than the law enforcers who lived like kings. What wonderful countries we had encountered since leaving Russia. We were fortunate, indeed, to have escaped the clutches of Russian communism.

Our happiness was regularly interrupted by attacks from the

partisans[8], not unlike what happened in Yugoslavia in the 1990s. It was horrific. They just came and killed women and children, not armed men, as they had no ethics, no honour, no rules at all. They just killed. Not that there is too much 'honour and ethics' in war. However, it is not a complete abandonment of being a human being if certain rules are applied. But not for the partisans, as they were a law unto themselves. In their thousands, they would attack a little village of farmers that perhaps had 50 soldiers and barbed wire for protection. My family and I were often caught on the wrong side of the barbed wire fence as the farm we worked on was on the outside of the protective fence. What saved us from slaughter and rape is that we spoke Russian and they assumed we were there as forced labour from the east. We understood their language as they understood ours.

One attack clearly imprinted in my memory was when we were inside the enclosure. We later heard that there were 6000 partisans on that occasion. We were in the A-shaped pine house. There were a lot of big and fierce explosions. Mother soon realised that if we stayed in the house, we would be incinerated. To get to a cellar we had to cross a considerable stretch of space where we would be fully exposed to partisan bullets, yet Mother insisted that it was worth a try. Only one person at a time could try their luck, as together we would make too big a target. All they had to do was throw a grenade and that would be the end of us. I remember being terribly frightened to go alone.

---

[8] World War II military operations in Yugoslavia began on 6 April 1941, when the nation was swiftly conquered by Axis forces and partitioned. Subsequently, a guerrilla liberation war was fought against the occupying forces and their locally established puppet regimes. Simultaneously, a multi-side civil war was waged between the Yugoslav communist partisans, the Serbian royalist Chetniks, the Croatian fascist Ustaše and Home Guard, Serbian Volunteer Corps and State Guard, as well as Slovene Home Guard troops. The human cost of the war was enormous. The number of war victims is still in dispute, but is generally agreed to have been at least one million.

Mother had no doubt this was the only way to go. She turned to my 14-year-old sister, Irma, and told her to go first.

"Show the little ones your courage," she said.

Irma looked at my mother confidently and said, "Tell me when, Mama."

On receiving the signal, she shot across the gap between us and the cellar without any hesitation. In the light of the explosions, we saw her on the other side, but she was not standing. She seemed in a heap and our hearts sank. Mother quickly sensed our panic and ordered my other sister, Lucya, to go. She did, and then they were both standing.

Mother then turned to the orphan girl and ordered her to go. She whimpered and protested, then went as instructed.

So, three were safe, and now it was just Mum and I. I stared in horror at her but all she said was, "This is the only way. When I tell you to go, you must go."

When Mum said "run," I did, blocking all my fears, and made it, but seeing Mum on the other side of the bullets terrified me. Up to this point in our lives, we had done everything together, the four of us seemed to function as one.

The traumas we had experienced together were of giant proportions, such as when the NKVD took my father prisoner, the persecution of Mum – we children being starved in the hope of breaking her spirit and all the time at the lowest possible ebb: we had faced all of these horrible experiences together. Yet here, we were separated by bullets. The fighting increased, momentum was high and there seemed to be no lull in the confrontation, so Mum just stood like a statue. We could not see her face, as she was too far away.

Suddenly I decided to run back, when I felt my sisters' grips either side of me.

"What good can you do by going back to Mum?" they said. "You will only make it harder for her to cross."

Logic did not come into it. I just wanted to be with Mum, to live or die. I did not want to be safe and alive without her. There was no let-up in the fighting. The night was lit up like daylight by all the explosions. We could see bullets flying as we stood there. We saw Mum leap into it all. This was more than 50 years ago and I still weep as I am writing. It was so horrendous.

She made it across, a miracle indeed. We held each other like drowning people, clinging to nothing more than hope. We moved away from the entrance of the cellar and deep into its darkness, falling over things and people, but we did not care as we were saved once again, and we were together.

The fighting went on until dawn. We were sure that this time all would be wiped out and then, as abruptly as it had started, the shooting stopped. A sudden silence fell upon the village. Eventually we ventured to the opening of the cellar and saw no one. We looked at the house and noticed a large black hole. We instantly thought of the widow inside with her six children. We waited a bit longer and word came that the partisans were retreating into the forest, but no one knew why.

When we went inside the house, we were not prepared for the sight that greeted us. That family, too, were huddled together, the five children in the arms of their dead 16-year-old sister, while the mother was walking around the room picking pieces of her daughter off the walls and floor. A hand grenade had landed on her lap. Her stomach was torn out, so she had not had a chance at all.

As we walked out onto the streets, we saw the reason for the partisans' retreat. On the edge of the trench lay a beautiful young woman, apples spilling from her shoulder bag, and she was dead. She did not look dead, just beautiful. She was the partisans' leader and, on learning of her death, they withdrew in grief.

The mother of six had gone into a world of such anguish and pain that she did not seem to be aware of anything or anyone except putting her dead daughter together in one piece. No one was allowed to enter the house. The remaining five children were also extremely traumatised and their mother could not comfort them. She did not seem to recognise them. The whole community, not just us, took them under their wings.

That very same day we all returned to our duties. The cows had to be milked, the fields worked. No one could predict when another attack would come. Time was very precious, so there was no time for grieving, no time to pause. We all had to jump at working extra hard to make up for lost time. We missed school that morning and went with the adults to the fields for the full day. The grieving mother was left to her own devices until the next morning, when her daughter had to be buried. It was all so unreal, so unlike the usual everyday life that it seemed like a dream. We wondered whether we were going to wake up and see it as the nightmare it was, but we realised slowly that it was not a dream, just simply a reality from which there was no escape.

Every night we had to be prepared for an attack, but as the days went by, we quickly returned to normal living and took chances by sleeping on the wrong side of the barbed wire fence and, yes, sometimes we did get caught between the two fiercely battling enemies. However, through the haze of trauma I can still see my beautiful mother, always calm and in control of our fate. Well, that was how I saw her. As long as I could see her calm face, nothing disturbed me or could hurt me. That's how I felt.

A very happy and joyful memory I have is of my mother returning from the fields at dusk, milking the cows and then coming to us, singing. By then it was really dark, yet she had no trouble cooking and, as the aromas reached our nostrils, we in turn were filled with joy in anticipation. The meals mum produced were magical, probably also because we were so hungry by the time they were ready. After eating, we quickly washed up, Mum got her guitar and we all sat very close to each other and sang into the night.

One night early in 1945, when we were in the cottage outside the fence, my mother whispered in my ear that the partisans were nearby. I froze with fear while listening to my mother's voice in the dark.

"We must go to the cellar of the big house," she said.

My sisters were safe, as they were elsewhere in the village. I was with Mum, and if she was going to die in this war then I, too, would like to die. We took something warm to wrap around us and made our way to the cellar. Inside, we stumbled over things. I remember falling over potatoes, as they are bumpy and it hurts when you fall on top of them. We finally reached the furthest depth of the cellar. It was like being bricked in on all sides. Mum found a place for us to sit.

"Put your head on my lap," Mum whispered. I did, and promptly fell asleep. I was with Mum, were my last thoughts. The love and confidence I had for my mother had no boundaries.

I woke to the sound and smell of burning. The whole cellar was lit up by it, too. I looked at my mother, who was very still, and I knew something pretty bad must be happening. She just told me to wait. The partisans had put straw against the walls of the house, poured petrol over it and set it alight. From the cellar door we could see the woodpile, which was also burning. We knew that the owner of the farm was hiding inside it. Mother just held my arm firmer but said nothing.

All of a sudden, the shooting stopped and the partisans retreated. Some partisans stood around the woodpile taunting the man and waiting for him to crawl out so they could kill him. It was so personal. They had known each other before the war and now they were boiling over with hatred. When Mum and I came out of the burning cellar they seemed genuinely shocked at the sight of a woman and a child. We addressed them in Russian and that saved our lives. They thought we were part of the forced labour scheme, which was quite extensive as far as Russia was concerned. The Russian workers were referred to as 'ost-arbeiter', or 'workforce from the east'. The partisans comforted us by telling us that the Russians were not too far away and would soon be here to save us. Little did they know what terror that created in our hearts.

The partisans received orders to retreat. As they did so, the farmer emerged from the woodpile, alight, but we managed to put the fire out with ease. He was shocked to the core, but his burns were not too serious. The three of us ran to the village, which was terribly battered. People were running in all directions, seemingly without purpose. On hearing that the Russians were close at hand, complete panic set in.

The Russians were advancing with considerable speed and soon the time came for us to be on the move once again. We each packed a bundle of food, only what each of us could carry, and one sunny morning we once again began our journey to freedom. We soon realised we should have set off earlier, as all of humanity seemed to be on the run from the evil of communism, hoping to reach the British sector.

Lina, mid 1940s

Chapter 6 – 1945, Austria

By the end of our first day, we came across a tidal wave of people, all heading in the same direction as us, towards the British sector. We could no longer walk of our own free will. When all moved, we moved. When all stopped, so did we. Apart from not getting on top of the other people and walking on their heads, there was nothing that could be done on our own initiative. We moved as a unit, not as individuals.

We walked into the night until we could not move another step, but there was little chance of sleep as the mass of people kept moving, stepping on or falling over each other. It was a tidal wave of humans moving constantly, as if nothing could stop it. When something obstructed the ones in front, we all had to stop.

Yugoslavia is very mountainous – the flat strip where we were was limited on one side by a mountain, and on the other by a deep ravine with a river at the bottom, so there was no way out of this situation other than to move or stop with the masses.

We did not rest for long, as we dared not get behind and take the risk of being caught by the Russians. We rested, we ate, had a little to drink and moved on.

I will always remember our first dawn on the road. It was so beautiful. The countryside was so picturesque. How could such evil as the Russian executions be happening in God's beautiful world? Mind you, I did not know God personally at that stage, all I knew was that there was horrendous evil that almost gobbled us up.

Once again, lice found their way to our heads. I hated the feel of them crawling about. They did not cause any pain from biting. This invasion was more psychological.

It does not take long to lose physical condition. In three days, we lost so much weight that we looked at each other in shock and horror. Where did the weight go so quickly? We had almost run out of food. It was all 'don't think, just move with the rest of humanity, move or be trodden underfoot'.

By dusk of the third day, we had reached the point of complete exhaustion and were looking for a spot, any spot in which to rest away from moving feet. Before that, though, we heard panic-stricken voices and word passed that Russian tanks were behind us. There was great fear that they would drive over all who could not get away, yet there was nowhere to go, no space anywhere.

People tried to surge forwards, but could not. Some fell, but the fear-driven people could not stop. They just walked over the fallen ones. The cause for the panic was someone spotting Russian tanks behind us.

Mother assessed the situation, came to a quick decision and quickly told us what to do. We were horrified at what she was saying, but there was no other choice. She told us to roll down the embankment straight to the bottom. We could hear the roar of the river below us. Mother said there might be a railway line by the river.

"Even if there is no railway line below for us to follow, drowning is preferable to being crushed by tanks or being taken back to Russia if we survive the tanks," she said after a moment of silence.

The orphan girl started sobbing. Mum wasted no time and told us to hold onto each other's hands and roll down the ravine together.

We stared at her and said, "What if there isn't a railway line? Then we will drown."

"Yes," she replied, "but that is better than being crushed by tanks, right?"

We trusted her implicitly. We got hold of each other's hands and jumped, then rolled down to the unknown. Would it be a big splash into a river or the blue metal of a railway line? We did not know, but held on to each other's hands and pure hope, nothing else.

We hit a railway line. The metal cut us rather badly, but we did not care. In fact, we did not feel pain at all. Instead, we felt the joy and hope of escaping a fate worse than death. We lay there stunned by the impact.

"And now we must run, run, not walk," Mum said.

By then none of us had footwear of any kind, but even with our bare feet on blue metal, none of us uttered another sound. We just ran, Mother in front. Then it occurred to us that the railway line might be mined. If it was, Mother would be blown up before our very eyes. However, running on sharp stones, cutting our feet, we were carried by something far worse, and the thought stayed for only a short length of time. All focus was on getting away from the terrorists. Run, run and run.

We covered 11 miles that way. My sisters almost carried me, one on each side. I was beyond fear, and all I wanted to do was to be left alone and keep still. My feet were bleeding, and I hadn't one ounce of energy left.

The railway line led to a village. Mother quickly established how far the Russians were from us and decided we could stop to rest and try to find some food. She left us at a barn while she went to the farmhouse and knocked on the door.

The farmer opened the door and Mum apologised and said, "I know you cannot feed every running person who knocks on your door, but we are at the end of our strength. Could we rest in your shed? We promise not to disturb the animals or cause any other problem for you. Please, just 'til the morning and we will be gone."

According to Mum, the farmer had tears in his eyes upon seeing us and just nodded his head. Mum assured us that somehow, she would find food in the morning. We huddled together for warmth and the farmer brought us a little food. We slept on straw, completely exhausted.

We awoke to the sound of Russian language and nearly died of shock. Had we gone through all this just to walk into another trap? No, it was not the front line Russians. It was the Vlasov army, which fought on the German side in the hope of ridding Russia of communism. They refused to put their arms down until they reached their destination, the British sector. Little did they know then that they would later be betrayed and handed back to the Russians. The British betrayal was a very shameful episode in history. Mind you, the Americans did the same. They called it 'repatriation'. At gunpoint? What hypocrisy.

When the soldiers heard us speak Russian, they picked we children up and put us on their wagons. Magically, food appeared. We must have looked a sight. Some soldiers hugged us, others just wept and swore. Our joy was short-lived, though, as orders soon came through from the General to say that civilians were not allowed to join the march, as it was an army. The soldiers were distraught but had to obey. At least they gave us food for a few days, during which we hoped to reach our destination, Klagenfurt, in Austria[9].

After eating and resting, we moved on. We were all worn out and

---

[9] Klagenfurt am Wörthersee, usually known as just Klagenfurt, is the capital of the federal state of Carinthia in Austria. During World War II, the city was bombed 41 times. Displaced persons began to appear in substantial numbers in the spring of 1945. Allied forces took them into their care by improvising shelter wherever it could be found. Accommodation primarily included former military barracks, but also children's summer camps, airports, hotels, castles, hospitals, private homes, even partially destroyed structures.

had blisters and cuts on our feet from the metal of the railway line, which made walking very painful, so we did not cover much distance that day. By then we were convinced that our efforts were futile, and that the communists would catch up with us next day. None of us spoke, yet we knew the other's thoughts. Our fate was clearly displayed as we were well aware of Russian tanks approaching from behind us, so there was no need for words.

As that day progressed, everyone around us was slowing down, too. It all became like slow motion. All looked back to see how close the Russian tanks were, knowing it was all just a matter of time before our fate was sealed.

Then a miracle happened. An ambulance stopped in front of us and a British soldier jumped out of the driver's seat, opened the back of the vehicle and gestured for us to get in. We froze: was he going to hand us over to the Russians? He came towards us, gesturing at the ambulance and, looking around to make sure no one had seen us, then all but pushed us in and closed the door. We just looked at each other and waited for an explanation. He drove on for quite some time before we were stopped. An armed soldier questioned the driver then moved to the back. We could see the door the handle turn, but then a second miracle. He did not open the back door, just waved the driver on. It was then that we burst into tears of relief, pain and hope at the same time.

We sat very close to each other as we heard Mother whisper, "We will make it. We have been saved."

Yes, we were saved. The driver took us all the way to Klagenfurt. When he stopped and opened the door for us, we could see great compassion on his face. All he said was, "I am so sorry. I am so sorry."

We later found out what those words meant. It was too dark for us to see the damage to the city from air raids, but the next morning revealed all. Very few buildings seemed in one piece. There were ruins everywhere. There was not one single whole building in sight and yet there were people everywhere. All were like us: in rags, barefoot and hungry. It was a pitiful sight, yet Mother reminded us that we had escaped a terrible fate. We must be happy and not despair.

"Something will happen, you will see," she said.

And happen it did, in the form of soup stalls dotted all over the streets – the 'ladleful of something' we could not identify, but it settled our hunger pangs. So that was a good beginning.

We found a corner in a bombed-out building. It had no roof, and the walls were jagged from the bombing. Mum and I went looking for something, anything that might help us to get through. It was terrible to see such beautiful things smashed, gorgeous tiles of all description in pieces. I had never seen such beauty and to see it smashed to pieces seemed such a tragedy and waste. Statues, pottery, furniture: nothing had escaped the raids and all was rubble.

But all that stayed with me only fleetingly. We had to find a means by which to survive. Seeing all the people around us who also had to survive, it seemed almost impossible. It was not just a few hundred, it was thousands and thousands of people. There seemed to be no space without hungry and dirty faces confronting us.

Mother was very calm, and this projected itself onto me, but not so to my sisters. They were older, so their perception was different to mine. Also, they had to be very, very careful because of the risk of rape. I looked more like a skinny child than the 13 years old that I was. Mother, too, was constantly conscious of the risk of rape. After all, she was only 37 or so and a very attractive woman. All these men in uniforms, straight from a five-year war, how could they suddenly become moral human beings? Most couldn't, and didn't.

The daily 'ladlefull of something' was just not enough. The British soldiers had plenty of food and soap, commodities which were very hard to come by. Little by little, though, the soldiers and some of the women found each other, and then those women were suddenly fed well and had soap to make clean themselves with.

Mother found a better way. She decided to go to the soldiers and offer to wash their clothes.

"Men are the same everywhere," she said. "No matter what their uniform. They don't like washing and ironing their clothes, so let us offer to do it for them."

People around just laughed and said, "Who will trust you with their belongings? You don't even speak their language. That's a stupid idea!"

Mum gathered up the courage to go to the army barracks. I was both embarrassed and frightened, but went with Mum as I did not want her to go alone. We got to the gates and tried to show them with our hands what we had come for. Eventually, they understood and led us to a laundry with soap and troughs. It was a beautiful sight. The thought of the convenience of it all and clean, running water was wonderful. I was delighted, and yet my mother shook her head and pointed to a gate. The soldiers pretended not to understand, made jokes and called out in friendly ways from barracks doorways. Yet my mother kept shaking her head and pointing to the gate. Eventually they agreed to give Mum some dirty washing and soap.

On arrival at our place of dwelling, I looked at Mum and pointed out that we had no utensils for washing clothes and no hot water. How were we going to do it?

Mum said, "We will find some buckets or something and then we will light a little fire to heat the water."

There was certainly plenty of firewood from the destroyed houses and broken furniture. Finding a bucket, or any metal container to hold water and heat up, though, proved to be almost impossible. There were plenty of utensils scattered everywhere, but they all had holes in them and it took us half a day to find something that did not leak, which was, of course, wonderful. We made our way back to our corner, lit a fire and proceeded with the chore at hand: washing shirts, trousers, socks, you name it, it was quite a pile of washing. While Mum was doing all that, she sent me to look for an iron.

"But Mum!" I lamented.

"You will find one, you will see," she said.

She was right. I had to work my way through many piles of debris but, behold, there was an iron, large as life. It was one of those irons you put coals into. I ran all the way back waving it in the air.

"You see? I told you would find one," she said.

To my surprise, she already had some garments spread out on top of the rubble to dry. We were so happy to be able to do the task. We also knew that the soldiers would give us food and soap and I could not wait to complete the washing and ironing. It was a really warm summer's day and everything dried quickly. Mum did the ironing on a broken door as I watched in amazement at how quickly she was getting through the load. My mother really knew how to work, no matter how many obstacles confronted her. They all simply became challenges to be overcome.

Before dark it was all finished. We each had a pile of beautifully folded clothing in our arms, stacked so high we could hardly see where we were going. On arrival at the gate, we caused quite a commotion as the soldiers saw us with their clean and ironed clothes. They shouted to each other and came running in wonder and then shook their heads and started clapping as they grinned from ear to ear. Mum and I gave them the clothes. We had no idea if they were the same people who had given them to us, but it did not seem to matter. They were so grateful but, most of all, seeing us in rags they had thought they would not see their clothes again.

How Mum wished she could speak English so she could tell them that having nothing does not mean you lack honour and honesty. I think they got the message anyway. But being only weeks since war ended, all were still in battle mode. Anything went: shooting, rape – so nobody felt secure, least of all women.

Back at the army gate, once again the soldiers pointed to the laundry and tried to persuade Mum to wash there. She shook her head vigorously and gestured for more washing. They rewarded us well with food and soap. Soap was so scarce you could exchange a cake of soap for almost anything. I skipped happily alongside Mum. Once more, she had found a way of feeding us and keeping us warm and safe.

So that became our salvation, washing and ironing for the troops. It did not take long for Klagenfurt to be filled with so many people that no amount of soup kitchens or bombed buildings could contain the flood of refugees, all fleeing communism. How anyone outside Russia could remain a communist seeing the tidal wave of running people is beyond understanding. Why Winston Churchill and Franklin Roosevelt allowed the Russians to set foot outside their borders is another puzzle.

Well, such is politics. It must have suited them to let the Russians chop up eastern Europe. All who could run, ran, from Poland, Hungary, Czechoslovakia and eastern Germany. Those were the places where this mass of people was coming from, as well as Russia.

The world authorities realised they had to move quickly before an outbreak of infectious diseases occurred. They quickly erected army camps, with 50 people per hut and 3000 in each camp. Truckload after truckload of refugees arrived.

We stayed in Klagenfurt until we were designated to a certain camp. Our first camp was in Spittal an der Drau, a town in the western part of the Austrian state of Carinthia, and another city affected by the war. Once again, we had to move. We were taken to our camp by truck, standing room only. Fortunately, Austria is not very large, therefore most journeys took only hours, not days.

On arrival, we saw a city of army barracks with narrow spaces between them for mobility. Double-decker beds lined each hut with little space between them. Two grey blankets per person were all the possessions we had. One blanket was used to separate each person from the stranger on the next bed, which was in order to fit more people per barrack: the beds stood touching each other. There were two potbellied stoves, one at either end of the barracks, but no fuel was supplied. That had to be found in the nearby forests.

We received a 'ladleful of something' per person, per day, and sometimes a slice of bread. We could never work out what was in the ladle, but it kept us alive.

The camps were multinational. Upon registering at the camp, we were each given a 'Displaced Person'[10] identification card. However, we were not prisoners – if any refugees wanted to find family and friends, they were free to move between camps.

---

[10] 'Displaced persons' camps in post-World War II Europe were established in Germany, Austria, and Italy, primarily for refugees from eastern Europe and for the former inmates of Nazi concentration camps. Two years after the end of World War II in Europe, some 850,000 people lived in displaced persons camps across Europe. The Allies categorised the refugees as 'displaced persons' and assigned responsibility for their care to the United Nations Relief and Rehabilitation Administration.

By now there were quite a number of men from eastern blocs, so it was no longer just women and children. It was pure chaos. What could be done with so many people that just kept on coming? They no sooner placed some when more came, like a tidal wave.

We also heard of Russians being allowed to come to the British or American sectors and they were emptying the camps at gunpoint, taking poor people back inside the Russian border and shooting them. The ones they did not shoot were told to march to Siberia. This was a constant fear for us. Was this the reason why we were brought here into a camp situation, just to make that task easier for the Russians?

One day we got a terrible fright when we saw Russian uniforms outside the barracks. On seeing that, people ran in panic, up a mountain or down a slope to a river. The panic was so horrendous that the British soldiers came and intervened, ordering the Russians out of the camp.

In recent years I have learned that more than two million people experienced this fate thanks to America and Britain's help, which is something else I cannot understand. How could they betray these people who had entrusted them with their lives?

Again, I have to focus on the opposite of evil, which in this case was a beautiful gentleman called Nikolai Tolstoy, an Englishman by birth. His father was Count Tolstoy, a descendant of Leo Tolstoy, who wrote *War And Peace*. He has written a book describing the events that occurred in Europe after 1945: 640 pages on crimes against humanity. The name of the book is *Victims Of Yalta*, and concerns Stalin, Churchill and Roosevelt betraying humanity at their meetings in Yalta. It saddens me immensely to name people who eventually took me to their countries and cultures. I even married a wonderful English-speaking man, yet this is how it was in Europe in 1945, a time when little made sense and Roosevelt and Churchill played power games at the expense of humanity. They forgot that the war had finished. They were still armed, as in war and did not know how to stop.

Everyone knew of the evil of Stalin, but no one expected the Allies to behave in the same way. All this is history, but if you want to know what really happened in those dark, miserable days in Europe, you should read *Victims Of Yalta* by Nikolai Tolstoy.

This man dedicated his life to the pursuit of truth. It led him to losing his house and his profession (he was a history scholar, a professor). He lost everything, yet said he would do it all again, as what he discovered was that important. Among the two million-plus people he wrote about were my mother's younger sister, Lydia, her husband and their two children, who were all untraceable. We've tried to track them down through the Red Cross and other avenues since the fall of communism, but they disappeared without trace. Solzhenitsyn said that 65 million innocent people fell at the hand of Russian communism and that it was not just under Stalin, but leaders that followed him.

As I remember it

Lina with her boyfriend, about 1948

Chapter 7 – Refugee camps in Austria

My mother and I were taken to a camp in Spittal an der Drau, a picturesque town nestled among mountains. The camp was two miles out of town. A train ran between Klagenfurt and Spittal an der Drau. My two sisters had married while in Klagenfurt, one aged 19, the other 16. I missed them terribly, especially as we were now split up, and no longer one unit.

Life in the camp did not have much order. The daily trip for the ladleful-per-person continued. When Mum noticed I was losing weight, she suggested I find my way to Klagenfurt.

"Vasa, Lucya's husband, always took care of me when I was within easy reach," she told me.

So, Mum coaxed me into catching a train. I had to walk those two miles or so in the dark, pitch black in fact, but Mother would say, "You will be all right, darling. If you stay here any longer you may not be strong enough to get to the station."

I was petrified, yet my trust in Mum was such that it left no room for doubt or to question her decision, so I went each time I needed to. The first time was the hardest. I was sure I would not make it and had to feel the way with my feet as I walked, all too frequently getting off the road into something prickly and rough. The relief I felt when getting on the train was immense. I closed my eyes and imagined the welcome I would receive from my sister – as I indeed got. They were so good to me! I would stay until they had fed me, then go back to the camp.

Mother also found another way of helping us to find food. She went to a farmer after he had harvested his potatoes and asked for his permission to dig again and collect any potatoes he had missed.

"But I didn't miss any!" he replied. "All this effort for so little."

"It will be something to nourish us," Mum said to him.

She was right. We had no shovels to dig with, just whatever we found. The farmer was right, though: he had harvested well and not many potatoes were left.

"If we get a bagful by the end of the day, it will feed us for a week," My mother said.

As usual, she was right. I must admit I got tired very quickly, so I would rest for a bit, then continue. Having nothing on us to eat at all didn't help. You get really hungry from physical labour. My mother's constant chatter helped me along, however. She was always so optimistic.

"We will be all right, I will find a way," she would say. "Wait until we get back to the camp. I will cook the potatoes and it will taste wonderful. Have another rest."

We found enough potatoes to feed us for about a week, and we could always go back for more when these were finished. We even hoped to find something that resembled a shovel to make digging easier.

I used to love watching my mother cook. She could turn anything into a delicious meal. In Yugoslavia, I delighted in watching her make noodles from big sheets of pastry as thin as can be, and without any rips. She would throw a sheet in the air and catch it. Come to think of it, everything my mother put her hand to happened as if by magic. She certainly was a multiskilled person who always worked with joy. Her motivation knew no boundaries.

I will not even try to describe refugee camp life, other than to say that when people have nothing to fill their days and no future to look forward to, it brings out the worst in a large percentage of them. Three thousand people, most bored stiff, in one camp and 50 in each army hut is certainly a recipe for disaster. There were regular bashings, even murders committed for no other reason than obtaining a packet of cigarettes.

Some of my time was taken up by school, such as it was, and my regular trips to Klagenfurt to visit Lucya broke the cycle of nothingness. Just waiting and waiting, and what for? No one knew.

I also started to look at the beautiful churches, of which there are many in Austria. The little ones appealed to me the most. I think the big ones overwhelmed me a bit, as they seemed more like museums or art galleries. I started to visit a little church within walking distance from the camp. I would walk in and stand at the very back, hoping no one would see me, and I would always leave before the end of the service, so that no one had a chance to talk to me. I felt so embarrassed, and I am still not sure why: perhaps of feeling that I did not belong anywhere. The little congregation looked so beautiful, like a happy family similar to us. But then, as Mum used to remind us, we also could have been gobbled up by the Kremlin gang, so we should be thankful for life and not grieve over what is lost.

Our potato-digging trips really saved our lives. The only trouble was that we had to move further and further away from the camp, which meant more distance to cover carrying the potatoes home. I remember an instance when we had had a fine 'harvest'. Our first farmer had given us two old shovels, so we found a lot more potatoes. At the end of the day, I could not lift the bag, so Mum put it on my shoulders and, for a while I was fine, but then my pace became slower and slower. As soon as Mum noticed this, she put her bag down and took mine off my shoulders and we would rest. I only wished that we had had something to eat, as I am sure we would have picked up pretty quickly. Instead, it seemed to make little difference.

After a while Mum would say, "Let's go so we get back before dark."

I knew what she meant. It was absolutely dangerous to be alone after dark, even for men. Women were, of course, far more vulnerable.

All the hardship was instantly forgotten once we returned to our barracks, though. We had potbellied stoves at each end of them, but wood had to be found to feed both of them. Mum was able to cook and I would watch her. My mother's voice was gentle and her chatter comforting. She made sense out of the most impossible situations and extended so much sympathy to me for having to work so hard collecting potatoes and getting wood. She could not have done either by herself. When collecting wood, one had to climb up the mountain while the other caught the wood at the bottom and, as it was always getting dark very quickly, we were running out of time and really had to rush. Once we returned to camp, though, it was pure joy just watching her cook while showering me with love.

So, between my brothers-in-law's efforts to feed me and the potatoes we collected, we were reasonably well fed. We also received little survival packages from the Red Cross, which were wonderful and included chocolate, which was better than gold as we could trade it for other essentials. Soap was almost impossible to get hold of, but, once again, Mum found a way around this. She put the ashes from the stove into a cloth and poured water through it. It was strong, and it made our hair fall out if we were not careful, but it kept our heads lice-free. When my brothers-in-law could get a cake of soap, it was treasured.

Both my brothers-in-law worked for the British troops. They only received food for themselves in payment, but somehow always managed to feed their wives and me at intervals.

Vasa, Lucya's husband, worked in a bakery. On leaving at the end of each day, they were all searched to make sure no bread was hidden inside their clothing, yet somehow, he had to get a little extra when I was staying with them. He got the bright idea of wrapping dough around his middle, thinking it would not be felt. Because of all the searching and stripping it took longer to exit.

One day, when a few people were found with hidden bread, a friend of Vasa's gazed at him and said, "Look at your tummy!"

The dough had started to rise due to his body heat. He ran to the toilet holding himself around the middle – it's a wonder no one else noticed! Once in the toilet he took the dough from his body, kneaded it really hard and kept an eye on the queue. When there seemed to be fewer people, he once again wrapped it around himself, dressed, and came out to be searched. He got away with it. My sister and I could not believe our good fortune to have bread to eat. Mind you, next morning I had to find a baker who wouldn't report us to bake the bread. There was only one place the dough could have come from and that was the British, as no one else had any. I was sent on that mission because they thought it was safer and that I wouldn't be arrested. I was so frightened, but could see no other way to ensure the baking. My brother-in-law certainly could not go, as he would get arrested immediately and my sister was with child, so, it all fell to me. Yes, I did find a baker who would bake the bread and not report us, but he would keep half of it.

"Never mind, better to have half a loaf than none," Mum said.

In those days, my brother-in-law was very thin. He had a good physique but was skinny. He was 19, same age as my sister, and had

had a pretty horrific time in his young life, but this made him a strong survivor, and a very skilful one. He would not let me starve.

Looking at him now, he could not smuggle an extra jumper on his body, let alone something bigger! He is well rounded and still as caring, and still has a good physique despite his roundness.

Lina, with her sisters' children, about 1948

On another occasion, with the help of a British officer, he 'acquired' many blocks of chocolate. By then, my sister had had her baby and somehow acquired a pram. We hid the chocolate in the pram (which weighed a ton!) under the baby, which was only a few weeks old. The chocolate was soon missed and everyone within a certain radius was searched, including us. While the searching took place, we all prayed that no one would touch the pram. The officer in charge loved babies, so he went straight over to the pram while we froze with fear. We thought he had been tipped off and knew the whereabouts of the chocolate. On finishing the search, the soldiers reported to the officer and he just touched the baby's hand as he leaned over the pram. We will never know if the officer had known about the chocolate and taken pity on us, the baby softening his heart, as he never said anything and simply left. The point of the chocolate was that we could exchange it for food. That night I went to sleep with a piece of chocolate in my hand.

For five years we went from refugee camp to refugee camp. In the third year, at the end of 1948, I received an offer to go for a suitability test to train in nursing. The camp hospitals were still full of wounded and maimed people from the war and had less than a skeleton staff to care for them, so the authorities decided to choose suitable young recruits to train on the job. I was so thrilled at being accepted – at last I would be doing something other than forever waiting.

By then I had filled out really well and, to my surprise, looked just like any other young woman. I had lost hope of ever becoming like my attractive sisters. I was the ugly duckling and yet, here I was, apparently a woman, at 16-and-a-half. Judging by responses from the opposite sex, I seemed to be developing really well. However, I had made up my mind not to be serious with anyone until I knew where we were going. I did not want my children to be born into camp life like my sisters' children, no way in the world.

It was exciting to be courted. On being accepted into nursing I was taken to another refugee camp, which had a large hospital. In a sense I was alone for the first time in my life, parted from Mother. She was very optimistic and encouraged me to go and learn. I was delighted to be part of something big – in my eyes nothing is bigger than taking care of the suffering. Nurturing was as natural to me as breathing.

We were tossed into the deep end from day one. During evenings we attended lectures, and at 6.00am we were back with the patients on the wards until whatever time. This was the pattern for six weeks. Some days we would finish between 6.00pm and 7.00pm. Quite often we went straight to a lecture, eating on the run.

I felt so deeply for the suffering of people. A lot of patients were from Russia, like me, and could not speak much German, so I became their interpreter. It was so exciting. I loved every minute of my time there, and I felt nursing was for me. The part of nursing I loved most was maternity. Babies were born as sure as humans' ability to love, and often people who were really desperate had children more frequently. That seemed to be their only link with life. I soon learned how to deliver babies, as the doctors rarely seemed to make it to the future mothers on time. To see a perfect baby arriving and holding it in my hands was pure ecstasy. They are so beautiful and perfect: miracles indeed.

I felt sorry for the mothers, as they had it really hard: there was no pain relief, just hard labour under terrible conditions. Often, they were left too long on hard tables with their legs in stirrups, waiting to be washed and/or stitched. There were just not enough doctors, so an awful lot was left up to we nurses, who had to deal with situations we knew nothing about, but it was us or no one. At our lectures, we would raise questions with doctors to clarify things, and to equip us better. What an exciting way to learn: we no sooner got the theory than we were deep into the practicing of it all.

Yet we still found time to go dancing or to the pictures. Sometimes our escorts had long waits, as we never knew when we would be finished, but they waited patiently. It took us five minutes to change from our uniforms into other clothes. On our way to town, we had to pass the British army camp and often there would be fights between the local boys and the soldiers, each resenting the other. On occasion it was more than resentment, simply outright hatred, which is understandable, as who wants to be occupied by foreign forces? No one.

Once in town we had a wonderful time, dancing, listening to music, enjoying each other's company and going for long walks by the river. It was simple but marvellous fun, and our youth did the rest. After all we had experienced, this was heaven. We had to be very careful of where we went out, though, and always did so in groups, never alone. Looking back now, I do feel sorry for those poor soldiers, as they too were in an unavoidable position. However, at the time it was frightening for us. After all, the troops were armed and the civilians were not. Needless to say, the situation was explosive and, from time to time, it did erupt and people got hurt or killed.

The time I spent there was unbelievable. The horrible things that happened there could not be excused by the label of 'war'. In many ways it was worse, for there were no rules. Every victor, every occupier, seemed to believe they were invincible and very much a law onto themselves.

One day, someone such as Nikolai Tolstoy, with his great writing skills and strong sense of right and wrong, comes along and writes many books on how things actually were. The impact of the situation was so immense, so complex: so many European races herded together with only one thing in common – the enemy, Russian communism. Millions of us were in little Austria alone.

Terrible decisions were made to bring Germany to its knees. Power games were played. Humanity did not come into it, as these dispossessed people were regarded as just being a nuisance, like flies to be brushed aside. Churchill, Roosevelt and a lot of other big shots knew what Stalin was like. Since the revolution, he had provided plenty of evidence of his evil aims. He had starved cities and eliminated most of Russia's intellectuals. My mother told me of foreign media filming frozen corpses in the streets. No way could the USA and Britain plead ignorance! Yet, they allowed Stalin into Europe, made him a friend and ally and continued with this until the iron curtain fell and the Cold War emerged.

I have strayed away from my own experiences into something else, something which I did not question at the time, when I just wanted to be happy. I wanted a country I could call my own. I knew Russia would not be the place for me as long as communism existed, and because of the way the Western world was helping Stalin to stay in power and destroy almost anything in his path. I did not expect this to change during my lifetime, but it did, even though it took more than 70 years to burn itself out.

Going back in time and place again to the camp, I spent more than two years living and working at the hospital and never tired of caring for the sick. My mother visited me occasionally, and sometimes I would get time off to visit my family, but that was not easy as the shortage of trained staff never eased. We had long days of work, 10 to 12 hours a day, seven days a week. The fulfilment I got out of my work outweighed the fatigue, though. As I got older, I started wonder how all of this was going to end. It was obvious it couldn't go indefinitely.

A lot of my friends emigrated to the USA, which seemed to be everyone's dream. After the Roosevelt experience, we were very surprised to find that his, wife, Eleanor, spoke on behalf of the refugees in Europe. She pleaded with the world on our behalf. She even came to Europe to see the state of everything for herself and was outraged by what she saw. This gave us a lot of hope. Many church congregations in the USA adopted whole families, took them into their country and built houses for them. This sounded like a fairy tale, but there were so many instances of this that we began to hope that all would change and we would, in time, also have the opportunity to start again somewhere else. My mother, my sisters and their husbands and I made a pact with each other that we would not let anyone divide us. We would wait for as long as it took, but not be parted. If and when we went to a new country, it would be together.

In early 1950 things started to move in the right direction. I received a letter from my mother urging me to come to her camp for an interview. It looked as if there was a country that wanted us. It wasn't America, but Australia. We knew nothing about Australia except that it was on the other side of the world. "All my friends went to America," was my first thought. Still, Mum said come, so I did.

There was one complication, though. I had been dating a young Austrian man for quite some time and did not realise how much we loved each other until now it seemed that we were likely to lose each other. His name was Maurice, although I called him 'Hanzie'. He was 19, and I was 18. I was a refugee, and he was an Austrian citizen. His family's roots were deep and he was its only son. When word came of the interview, I had no time to return to his city or my hospital because things started to move very quickly. So, I wrote to him. He got on the next train and came to join me, insisting that he would also travel to Australia.

"Hanzie, you can't do this to your parents," I said. "You are all they have."

He was adamant that he was not going to let me go. I pleaded with him to return home, but the only way he would go back was if I promised to go with him and meet his parents.

"I am sure they will love you as much as I do," he kept saying.

"But Hanzie, if I am not prepared to part from my family, how can I expect you to do this?"

"I am making this decision, not you," he persisted. "It is my choice to follow you to the end of the world."

"But, Hanzie, that is exactly where I am going. Four weeks of ship travel is a long, long way from home."

It was like speaking to a deaf person. He just continued pleading with me to go and meet his parents. Well, I did go, and it was one of the saddest days I'd experienced in a long while. His parents were very nice and made me feel very welcome, but they were reeling from the shock of being told their son wanted to leave them for good. Travel was very difficult in those days, so once people landed somewhere, that was largely where they stayed for the rest of their lives.

His parents just walked around in utter anguish. They hardly spoke to me or to each other. Hanzie would constantly look for opportunities to be alone with me and hold me in his big strong arms. He was a professional boxer, which was something else his parents were trying to stop him from being involved in before he got brain damaged. Boxing in the 1940s and '50s had few rules and certainly no protective head gear.

"Lina, it will be all right, you will see," Hanzie said. "They will get over it, as long as we hold on to each other."

When he held me, I also became confident that somehow it would all work out. But this confidence only lasted until I laid eyes on his parents. My heart went out to them, and I could see in their faces a plea and a statement as if to say, "You can change all this by just leaving."

When I went to bed in Hanzie's parents' home during that episode, sleep did not come easily: I just lay there staring into the night sky. I could make out the church in the distance and the tall pine trees then, suddenly, a hand touched me gently on the face. It was Hanzie. My bed was the top one of a bunk bed and he was standing on a stool so his face was level with mine. As he gently stroked my face, I felt his strong hand tremble. I begged him to go, but he would not.

"Do you realise, my love, that this might be the last time we ever see each other?" he said.

Then we both cried a little and he placed his head on my chest and said, 'Hey, I can hear your heartbeat."

Fortunately, our love was pure and platonic. I had seen too many babies being aborted while nursing and the possibility of getting pregnant terrified me. So, we just held each other, which was dramatic enough. I knew that I could never part from my family and, if he and I had made love, I could not have parted from him. So, it was not even a temptation – it was an impossibility as far as I was concerned. The power of his arms around me gave me strength. How long we held each other for I have no way of knowing, but eventually he had to go. I stayed awake most of the night.

His mother walked through the room occasionally. I am sure she was just as afraid of something happening that might make the situation irreversible. I wanted to speak to her, but could not. What could I say, seeing that I could not promise her that I would get out of Hanzie's life? My pity for her was great, but I had my limits, too, and at that point it was beyond me to say I would let him go forever.

Next morning, the house was like a wake at a morgue. Hanzie and I tried to eat, unsuccessfully. When I left to go to the train station, they just stood on the porch of their beautiful, centuries-old house – the house intended for Hanzie and his children – and looked pleadingly at me. Hanzie tucked me under his arm as we walked off with the confidence of the very young and in love.

"Wherever you go, I will follow," he kept saying. For him, there was no question of us losing each other, end of story. I did not share his confidence of not losing each other. I could not get rid of the faces of his parents in my mind.

I promised to inform him about our departure as soon as I knew something. Which I did, and he was with us that same day. My sisters and their husbands asked us to come with them to a guesthouse for the evening, and we did. We just did not know what else to do with ourselves. The atmosphere inside the guesthouse was very friendly and happy. A big band played non-stop and we soon became happy and confident about the future. We danced a lot or just sat close to each other.

The next day, urged by me, Hanzie went back home and soon we were ordered to move on to Bremen harbour in north-east Germany. I thought my heart was broken beyond repair, but deep in my heart I knew I could not be happy at the expense of two other people whose lives would have been shattered.

Within easy reach of Bremer harbour, we waited for six months for a ship to take us to Australia. Hanzie and I corresponded frequently. His letters were so powerful, so reassuring, and then *Skaugum III* arrived to take us across the oceans and seas. It was both frightening and exciting.

We had another sadness to take with us. My sister Irma's four-year-old son was found to have a shadow over his lungs and they were refused visas. Australia was very strict about keeping TB away. We were shattered and did not know what to do. We wanted to stay, too, but we no longer qualified for refugee camp status since we had been re-categorised as 'placed people', among those who had been accepted by and into another country. We were told the decision was irreversible. We all sat down and talked it out, and it seemed that the best thing was for us to get a foot in the door by going and then working towards bringing my sister and her family out later. It was a complication we could have done without, though.

As soon as we boarded the ship, I reported to the vessel's hospital head offering my services on a voluntary basis. There was no money to pay me, but I was happy to be helping the unwell. The evening we left Bremen was 25 August 1950, which was my birthday, when I turned 19. I sat at a porthole watching lights disappearing in the distance as our ship gained speed until I could no longer see the lights and there was just a big black hole before my eyes.

*The assembled family prior to departure in 1950.
Lina and her sisters have linked arms at the front*

I left my home country without even getting to know it even a little. I am Russian born and of German ancestry: the Volga Germans, as we were called, or 'volks Deutsche' by origin. In old countries such as Russia, being born there does not make you Russian. People retained their racial identity. My ancestry dates back to 1750, and yet we were still regarded as German by the Russians. As I looked out through the porthole, I reflected that Russia was the country of my genetic roots. I had only seen it war-torn and destroyed by allied armies. I wished then that I could have known it in times of peace and dignity. All the wonderful stories I had heard about German people lay in in ashes of war, of losing that war and being occupied. Not a pretty sight at all. Disaster heaped upon disaster.

Chapter 8 – Arrival in Australia

I did not brood for long as I was too excited. So much was happening, and so quickly, that I could not keep still for long. I went from one experience to another constantly, giving myself no time to reflect. What was there to think about? I was going to a country the other side of the world. I knew I could not speak their language, and not a single friend was going with us, as all my friends went to America. It was pretty scary, yet my mother kept reminding me of our choices – refugee camps or Russia – and neither was acceptable.

"You will make new friends," she always said. "This is a new land we are heading for where people are not affected by European traumas.

"Here is a country that is giving us a new start, another chance of making something of our lives, and we must not let it down, or ourselves. We must try to leave as many of our traumas behind as possible. Only then can we make a new start. We must give ourselves completely to this new land and, above all, not try to change the things we cannot change. If we don't accept the difference, it will not work, and we will only disappoint the people of this land and let ourselves down."

These were my mother's strong words of advice.

"Be happy," she concluded.

As the shore lights of Bremen faded to nothingness my attention went elsewhere. I went to the ship's hospital and already there were quite a number of seasick people. There were others who were ailing, too, but they somehow managed to hide it and did not come to the hospital until we were a long way from shore. Generally, we dealt mainly with seasickness. After all, we had been thoroughly screened before being accepted for immigration and only the young and healthy had qualified.

That first night I stayed up late as we were quite busy at the hospital, but I also didn't want my birthday to end. I was now 19 and on the way to a new country whose language I did not speak, but that did not discourage me.

I tried very hard not to think about Hanzie, and when I did, I told myself that our parting was only temporary. I wrote to him each day, at first anyway. It was so good to have my sister and her family around and, of course, Mum. She was very quiet and withdrawn. It reminded me of the time when my little brother died, but this time it was different. This time she talked about the beautiful life we would make for ourselves in this new country and then we would bring my other sister, Irma, out to join us.

Leaving Irma behind with an unwell child was devastating. While we were together, we had planned to emigrate as a party of five young workers, two children and only one dependent person, Mum. At the age of 44, Mother no longer qualified as a worker, therefore she could not emigrate in her own right and also had to be signed for by all of us. Now, everything was different: Mum was allowed to travel with three young workers and two children. But my sister was left behind without support or guarantee of eventually being allowed to travel. They were on their own with a child that had a shadow on its lungs.

I enjoyed the trip immensely. I was very, very busy at the hospital and the first officer took me under his wing. He was 30, which seemed old to me, but I felt quite safe in his care and enjoyed the attention while other females looked on with envy; which was very flattering. As time passed, I noticed a change in his attitude towards me, so I tackled him and asked him if he was married. After all, he was old enough to be married. He was honest enough to tell me that, yes, he was married, but qualified for divorce. I told him this sounded too complicated for me. He said he understood and showed me a photograph of his three-year-old child.

I must give him full marks for being a gentleman. He treated me nicely, but not in a courting manner. He left the pace up to me, which suited me very well. One way or another I saw him every day during the four weeks it took to get to Fremantle, Western Australia. Sometimes we would just stand on deck leaning on a rail, fantasising about life, or simply saying nothing. When we reached our destination, we exchanged addresses. Actually, he gave me his address in Denmark. I did not have one.

In December 1950, Fremantle seemed like a very small affair. We were wondering what else there was to this new land of ours. Next stop was the Northam army camp, about 50 miles north-east of Fremantle. Even though it was only the end of September, for us it was extremely hot. Maybe it was in contrast to the cold we came from, but it was a bit of a shock to the system and made us wonder what summer would be like if it was already that hot in Spring. Still, we were here to stay and must make the best of it.

I did not stay in the camp for long as, to my delight, I was quickly placed into the workforce. My workplace was an old people's home in Shenton Park, Perth, where there is a rehabilitation centre now, but back then it was called Carinia. I loved it. The old people were so kind to we refugees who could not speak English. They told us they had never been treated with as much kindness and respect as they received from us. This worked both ways, though. We were nice to them and, in return, they repaid us doubly in terms of love and helping us with our learning to speak English. They did not mind how many mistakes we made, as they simply quietly and patiently corrected us.

I loved them all, but some stand out in my memory, such as Mrs Bell, who was a tiny, delicate person with a body riddled with arthritis. Her every joint was twisted and she was in a lot of pain. Nurses, always in a hurry, caused her unbelievable extra pain. From my first contact with Mrs Bell, she recognised my ability to empathise with others. Her speech, too, was halting and slurred.

The first time I bathed her I was extremely careful while laying her in a bathtub, then held her for as long as she wanted me to. Letting out the bathwater I had to get down on my knees to wipe her dry. She was so light, like a child. I half-dressed her in the bath so as to minimise movement and then ever so slowly, lifted her into a wheelchair and got off my knees. She always gave a big sigh of relief and then tried to smile, but that, too, turned into a grimace. On completing her bathing, ready for the day or night, depending on my shift, she tried hard to hold my hand, but hers shook so much that even that was not possible. She probably had Parkinson's disease as well as arthritis. Beautiful Mrs Bell, I am sure she is an angel now. She was so patient, despite all her pain, so kind. She always tried to smile at everyone through a veil of pain.

I worked at Mt Henry (also in Perth) for about 18 months, after Carinia was shifted there into a new, sterile environment that had no privacy. The new wards had glass partitions from the waist up so the nurses could see into whole wards at a glance, which was good for the nurses but made dummies out of the patients. They, too, could see from one end of a ward to the other. No one had any privacy at all, and they resented being on show and dehumanised. It was all structured for the convenience of the staff, like a paddock for sheep.

The community was so proud of its contribution to the elderly, but did not realise that this was not what they needed. They needed to be loved, to be part of a community and humanity, not bought by big spending and then forgotten. I did not know that worse was yet to come, however, when I got sent to Claremont Mental Hospital in Perth.

In the meantime, the water supply authorities had constructed a nice camp in Kelmscott in greater south-east Perth for its workers. Most new arrivals were now working in water supply projects as labourers. My family was delighted to be together yet again. Our rent was one pound a week, which seemed reasonable at the time, but come to think of it, represented one quarter of our wage. Well, beggars can't be choosers was our philosophy and we were supplied with army blankets.

With my first wages I bought Mother a doona so she did not have to use the army blanket any longer. I had to put it on lay-by as the price was three weeks' wages. I wanted to spoil my mother. A few months later I put a Singer sewing machine on lay-by; nothing but the best for Mum. The sewing machine cost 60 pounds, so took quite a while to save up for. The third thing I bought was a sewing machine for myself, but this was a second-hand one for 40 pounds. It took so long to sew by hand, particularly the long seams. Compared to that, a machine was very fast.

It was camp life with a difference. We all had a nice hut per family. Not 50 people in one barrack as we had experienced in the British refugee camps. For the first time since before the war started, we had privacy. The soil in Kelmscott was beautiful, and it grew anything we put into the ground and watered. It did not take long for the huts to be swallowed up by sweet corn and almost every other vegetable under the sun. Wonderful! We began to feel like ordinary people, not refugees.

As I remember it

My life at Mt Henry was very happy. I did not have to work 10-15 hours a day and I had plenty of spare time. I loved going dancing with friends, and to the beach and, on days off, to see Mum in Kelmscott. Hanzie and I were still corresponding. We continued longing to be together but, as time went by, I realised this was only a dream, and began to feel sure that I would never see him again. Still, we needed each other. We could not shut the door.

I met a really nice man called Joseph. He was Hungarian, a doctor and, as I later found out, a married man. Separated, but married just the same. Once I found out he was married, after dating him for about six months, I refused to continue seeing him. He was the one who insisted on taking me home one night after going out and he ended up missing the last bus back to Perth.

I tried to stop him from doing this, but he just said, "I always take my ladies home to their parents' house."

Later, he told me how many lampposts there were between Kelmscott and the Causeway, where the first bus picked him up. He pleaded with me not to break it off as he and his wife had been terribly unhappy for years and had been separated for three of them, but I just could not jump that hurdle – a married man! It was beyond me.

As it turned out I met him at a department store one day soon after I was married. He greeted me in a very cordial manner, then took my left hand in his, looked at my third finger and said, "Married?" I said, "Yes".

"Well, well, you are married, and I am divorced," he said.

"Joseph, I am very, very happy and in love with my husband," I said.

He let my hand go and said, "I can see that."

Our paths never crossed again. I never heard anything from him, or knew how his life evolved. It is strange how you start reliving your youth as you get older and remember the people who had had a strong impact on you.

Twelve months after our arrival in Fremantle my sister Irma, still in a refugee camp in Austria, finally had an opportunity to emigrate. We were ecstatic. We found out that, although the shadow on the lungs of her son had gone, the boy was not really strong enough to undertake the journey. She asked the doctor what she needed to do to give him a good chance of making it and the doctor told her not to keep him where there were lots of people. He needed plenty of fresh air, not other people's breath, because that would knock his immunity to pieces and the shadow would return. If it did, he would not be allowed to set foot on Australian soil and the return journey would kill him. Without hesitation my sister said she would take the chance.

"I know we will make it," she said. "Fresh air is the one thing I know I can provide for him."

When the doctor asked her how, she replied she would place herself and her child on the top deck of the ship and that they would not budge until they reached Australia. The doctor shook his head and said it was up to her, but he didn't fancy her chances.

"What chance do I have here?" my sister said. "Rot in the camp? No, I am going and that is that."

She had to sign for her son so the doctor would not be held responsible for his fate. We received a letter informing us of their journey that would reunite us.

The ship they boarded was a former aircraft carrier without cabins, just one big line of bunk beds filled to the brim with people. When some were seasick it created a terrible stench, and no one seemed to be able to clean up quickly enough, so the smell made others sick as well.

My sister soon realised the meaning of the doctor's words. She really had no idea it would be that bad. She found a corner on the deck which had a little bit of shelter for herself and the boy.

"Well, my little one," she said. "This is where we are going to stay until we reach Australia."

At night, the sailors tried to persuade her to go below to sleep, but she refused. Her husband brought food for them and they only left their spot when they had to relieve themselves.

When the winds were strong, the sailors tied her and her son to something heavy so they would not get washed overboard. Everyone thought she was mad, but she became convinced that going down below to the mass of people and the stench would kill her son, so she stayed outside. She could hear the doctor's words going around and around in her head.

"He will never make it," the doctor had said.

"Yes, we will, my little one, yes we will," she kept saying.

This is how my sister came to Australia. Her husband was wonderful and did all he could to help, but it was mostly a one-person vigil by my sister and the life of her son.

On arrival in Fremantle, they were shocked to hear that WA had enough refugees and that they had to go to Victoria. No one was allowed to disembark. She pleaded with the authorities, but to no avail. The powers on board would have done anything to help this determined mother who had run a marathon, so to speak, but it was not up to them. My sister cried with frustration. Melbourne was on the other side of Australia.

"How will I find them?" she lamented to herself.

When we learned that the ship had not been allowed to stop in Fremantle, we, too, wondered just how she was going to find us, so we waited eagerly to hear from her.

On reaching Melbourne, they were placed in an army camp. Her husband had work immediately as, like us, he was under contract to work for two years wherever he was sent, so was placed soon after their arrival.

It took them some time to earn enough money for the journey across Australia. Irma's husband wanted to stay in Melbourne a little longer as he liked his job as an assistant cook, but my sister had had enough of being alone and her little one was not very happy, either.

"Misha, I am going to WA to look for my family," she told her husband.

She hardly spoke a word of English, but she managed to by a train ticket to Perth, though she did have a little trouble understanding a man who kept saying, "Single or return?"

She knew what single meant, the opposite of married, but did not understand the rest of the conversation.

"Perth, Western Australia," she said, quickly adding, "One".

She got quite indignant. "What business is it of theirs if I am single or married?" she said later.

She bought the ticket, holding the hand of her son. "The cheek of him," she thought. Later, when she found out the meaning of 'single or return', she felt quite badly about her annoyance with the man.

Arriving at Perth railway station, she just stood there in a bit of a panic. "Where to now?" she thought, then, "A taxi will find them." She walked to a taxi and showed the driver a five-pound note and the address she sought, pointed to the money and said, "That is all."

The taxi driver smiled, said "Yes, yes," and pointed to the back seat.

She got in after giving him the cash and this is how she arrived at the Kelmscott water supply board-hut camp. When she arrived that morning, it was on my day off, so I was there, too. When we saw the taxi, we looked in wonder. Who could possibly be coming to this camp in a taxi? Then it stopped in the middle of the rows of huts so they could look both ways to the end of the street. Everyone in the camp was outside their huts by the time she got out of the cab.

We could not believe our eyes. I ran towards Irma, but Mum just stood there, unable to move, as if cemented to the ground. Even when we reached Irma, Mum seemed lifeless. All four of us embraced. The men were at work and the multitude of people who followed us to our hut rejoiced in our reunion. We laughed, we cried, we talked, all four of us at once. What a day. We had really thought we would never see each other again, and here we were together.

My sister's husband stayed in Melbourne a bit longer to earn some more money, but he followed her not long afterwards. I soon found a job for my sister, at Mt Henry, of course. It was so great to have her with me.

Mt Henry and all we experienced was magic. Irma was just as kind to the old folks as I and received just as much love from the elderly residents. But the entire situation puzzled us no end. The Australian girls we encountered at work and the visitors who came to visit their parents were so extremely nice, so what were all these old people doing in a home?

We felt they should be with their loved ones and be a part of their lives, seeing the people they love every day, not just once a week, fortnight or month. Some of the residents never received any visitors at all and we simply could not understand this. Where we came from, the aged were special people from whom you sought advice, to whom children turned to when Mum and Dad were too busy and, of course, the young looked after the old just as the old had looked after them when they were little and helpless. There were so many things to adjust to in this new country, apart from learning a foreign language, but this matter seemed so very tragic. All these people with so much to give and no one to give it to.

The assembled family at the Nissan hut in Kelmscott, about 1953.

After one year at Mt Henry, some retrenchment of staff took place and my sister Irma was one of those who lost their job. I was shocked and asked the matron what she had done wrong to lose her job. "Nothing," our matron replied.

"Then why does she have to go?" I inquired. My English was still too limited to understand retrenchment, so I said to the matron, "If my sister goes, I too go."

She shook her head, telling me I did not have to leave, but I repeated, "If my sister goes, I too will go," and we did. We left Mt Henry together and began a search for new employment.

This turned out to be more difficult than either of us had expected. That is the optimism of youth. Our English was limited, yet we were confident about getting jobs, seeing as we were prepared to work extremely hard.

Irma and I walked out of Mt Henry with no new jobs in store. Finally, we went to a place where there was a chronic shortage of staff: Claremont Mental Asylum, which is now known as Graylands Hospital. To me, 'Claremont' is still the tragic word for lost people.

In the 1950s, if there was a person no one knew what to do with, they were committed to Claremont. A lot of alcoholics ended up there. If a mother grieved too long over the death of a child, she ran the risk of being classified as 'mentally ill'.

If I had regarded Mt Henry was tragic, Claremont was unbelievably appalling. We were employed immediately and were also, for reasons unknown to us, put into the most violent ward, Ward II. Ken Kesey's novel *One Flew Over The Cuckoo's Nest*, and the subsequent film version, depict this sort of environment pretty well. Every day we worked under lock and key and the staff had master keys. When a patient lost all control and was violent, he or she was put into a canvas straitjacket, then placed in a padded cell. Yes, that is exactly how it was.

In those days there were not many drugs available for treatment of the mentally unwell and, when all else failed, shock treatment was carried out. Those who had already experienced shock treatment resisted with all their might and one woman in that state had the strength of two men, so it was extremely difficult to get them to the table for treatment. They were then strapped down, and a rubber bit put in their mouths so they would not break their teeth or bite off their tongues in the ensuing fits of anger.

It was so inhumane, so unbelievably sad. The nurses who had been there for a while told us we would get used to it, and they were right. To my surprise I learned skills that enabled me to cope as I gained experience, but I never got used to it.

My sister got beaten up rather badly by a patient who had begged her to go alone with her somewhere. She broke the rule of never being out of sight of another staff member. Quite some time had passed before we noticed that she was missing, as we were busy organising this and that for the patients, all 200 of them. Once we realised my sister was missing, we went into a blind panic. It took us quite some time to find her, as she was in a deep valley at the end of the yard. A tall fence obscured her, so deep was the dip, and there she was alone with a violent patient beating her. By the time we found her she was on the ground, certain this patient would kill her. Three people raced down the slope to grab the patient while I ran down to make sure my sister was alive.

It was reported to the matron, who just said, "You should not have been alone with a patient."

She did not even ask about any damage was done to my sister, and seemed much more concerned about the patient! I think the matron had been at Claremont for far too long and, in many ways, she was more like one of the patients. My sister had to go and see a doctor, as she was badly hurt.

He gave her one look and said, "Good heavens, you look like a road roller went over you."

He checked her over and found no broken bones, but said that she would take some time to heal. He gave her two weeks off and told her to come back then for further assessment.

We worked at Claremont for almost two years, and it was like another world. Meal times were the worst of all with food flying like missiles. We had to be ready to duck at all times. Fortunately, the patients tended to aim at each other instead of the staff.

To get a hundred patients out into the yard at the same time was almost impossible, as fights broke out when we forced them out against their will. We were considerably understaffed all the time and, besides, how could we reach that many people? It was really frightening to see such a large slice of humanity in such complete confusion. I tried to be near a door with a key in my hand, ready to unlock it and run, but that was not always possible.

Youth was one factor that made it possible for me to cope with working at Claremont. No way could I work there now or at any other time in my life. I had my sister with me, not that we were always on duty at the same time or in the same ward, but it was great when we were and we saw each other at meal times and often after work.

Lina, in her nurse's uniform.

Chapter 9 – Marriage

It was when I was working at Claremont that Andrew came into my life. I liked him instantly, but felt I could not respond to him as I could not yet speak much English and besides, I was already engaged to be married.

My fiancé was in Darwin, constructing pre-fabricated houses. I think he came from Austria and, together with a few hundred other skilled men, had been brought to WA for this purpose. Most of them ended up staying after the end of their contract.

Andrew quickly picked up on my reluctance to associate with him and asked me why.

"Two reasons," I told him. "First, I am engaged and secondly, I don't speak English and you don't speak Russian or German."

"You said that very well," he replied. "English you can learn, and engaged is not married."

I held back for quite some time. He became quite well known to the staff members as they answered the doorbell.

"Hey, how come he keeps coming here?" someone would ask. "He is not a foreigner. He is Australian and you can't speak much English."

I got a bit annoyed with this, so I said, "Why do you ask me? Ask him next time you go and answer the door."

We were behind locked doors, so no one could just come to visit a staff member, as they had to ring the main doorbell, give their name and wait to be told if the staff member they were looking for was present or not. The nurses' quarters were a little distance away from the patients' wards, so we could not hear them, but, nevertheless, we were still locked in.

Before I start on Andrew and my courtship and a love that led to the marriage of a lifetime and constant love, I had better find the courage to tell the story of my fiancé.

He was an Austrian soccer player and also must have been a very skilled construction worker seeing that he was brought all the way to Australia from his homeland. He was handsome and always had a bit of stray hair falling over his forehead. He was of medium height, under six foot, but tall enough for me to be wearing high heels and still be shorter than him.

We had met at a dance and, as soon as our eyes met, I felt in my heart I could let Hanzie go. I wrote Hanzie a letter telling him to fall in love with someone else and not to cross the sea and destroy his parents. I surprised myself with this objectivity, but then I closed my eyes and saw the face of the stranger and knew that if it was not him, it would be someone else. It convinced me that I could love again, and I could let Hanzie go. After all, two years had gone by since we parted, time enough to heal, I guess.

The stranger's name was Franz and, to this day, I don't know how he traced me all the way to Claremont after meeting me at that dance. My name was called to say that he was at the door and there he stood after I unlocked it. I was still in my nurse uniform.

He gave a little shy smile and said, "Shall we go to the nearest milk bar?"

"Yes", I replied,

For the next three months I saw him daily. I would come off duty and there he would be. How he knew which shift I was on I have no idea.

Talk about 'where there is a will there's a way'! I was in heaven. All I had wanted to do all my life was to grow up, fall in love and have lots and lots of children and I was sure this was my dream.

I don't know why it should be that more than 40 years later it should matter how I lived and felt at that time. Yet somehow it is like another time, which needs to be acknowledged so we can learn from it. All I know is that, without meaning to, I broke Franz's heart. I have no doubt at all that I married the right person for the right reasons, so why the sadness now? I believe that any pain we inflict on others leaves a residue of sadness for that which was unresolved. Also, I heard that he had a tragic life: in what way I don't know and that, too, made me feel bad. It would have been nice if he had also found the love, joy and fulfilment I did.

But now it was Andrew who was ringing the doorbell at Claremont and waiting for me to be called. I can still see him standing before me on opening the door, all tall, dark and handsome. Well, a lot more than handsome – there was something special about him. He invited me out and I kept refusing.

"I can't, I am sorry, but I just can't," I would say.

"Don't you like me?" he would ask.

"No, that is not the reason,' I'd reply.

It began very differently from how I had always imagined it would be when I met the man who would become my husband, but at that time I was sure that the man of my life was in Darwin. The more I saw of this stranger, the more perplexed I became. I also saw him in church, as he was my pastor's son. I disappeared from church before services were over because I did not want people to put themselves out on my behalf. I was also embarrassed about my limited English and, of course, I did not know how to handle this stranger called

Andrew. His parents were exceptionally kind to me, and I loved them from the very start. How can anything become so complicated when all you want to do is to fall in love, marry and have children? This was what I had always wanted, so why this difficulty?

So, I kept my distance from everyone at church. I loved going to church, but Andrew being there made it awkward. One day I heard a very nice deep voice singing right behind me in church and I could not resist the temptation to look behind me. Our faces almost touched he was so close – he must have been leaning forward as I turned. I smiled as I looked into those beautiful dark brown eyes. Yes, it was Andrew.

I was very conscious of his presence. That day I left the church even more quickly than usual. What was happening to me? I felt like asking someone, but whom? Well, after a while I asked my sister Irma what to do.

"It wouldn't do any harm if you went out with him and got to know him a bit better," she said. "And then you tell him he cannot court you and why. It's that simple."

"So why was it not that simple for me?" I asked.

Well, that was how I found my love for life and now, more than 40 years later, I am still in love with him. I am sad that this love had a beginning of such complexity, but it seemed that someone had to pay a price and that was Franz. Once I wrote to Franz to tell him that I was marrying Andrew, our communication ceased. I got swept along by the tidal wave of love and joy. I told myself I would never look back on my youth, my search for love and roots, and I would only look ahead.

Andrew, being Australian, made me see Australia in a different light. The love that came my way from his parents, plus the love that flowed between my sisters, their husbands and my mother and

Andrew was magical. My family lived in the water supply camp in Kelmscott at that time, the 'Silver City' as someone named it. Both my sisters and their husbands were employed full-time while my mother took care of their children. They also worked on weekends whenever they could. They worked very, very hard, yet they were full of happiness and optimism for getting on their feet and giving their children better opportunities in life. This was their goal, their motivation and they fulfilled it.

Andrew's love swept me along like a river in full flow. There was no room for doubt, for anything but love. I call it 'the joy of Andrew'. I was sad it had not an ideal beginning, but I was so happy that not even the Franz experience could dampen my spirit.

"He will be all right," I kept saying to myself. "He is young, he is handsome, he will find someone else to love and I will be just a memory."

On one of our visits to my family at Kelmscott at the end of the summer of 1953, it was harvest time. Mum had married again, for a fourth time. Her new husband's name was Michael Zornick and he was a Russian-born Cossack who had served in the British army during World War II. My stepfather grew beautiful sweet corn. Mother decided to cook a big pot full of it and place it on the table for Andrew's visit. My eldest sister, Lucya, was distraught.

"But, Mum, it looks so peasant-like," she said "What will Andrew think of us? You can't do that!"

Mum was just as adamant that if he was going to be offended by a 'peasant-like sight', then he better find out now, before the courting got too serious. All this was unknown to me as we arrived. Andrew, on seeing the large bowl of his favourite food – until then he had only ever seen one cob at a time – nearly fainted with pleasure. We all relaxed and had a wonderful time, and the lack of common language did not seem to hinder us in any way at all. My mother spoke no English at all and my sisters and their husbands only had a survival vocabulary, but this did not matter as there was so much joy. I felt our love must have spilt over to our families and it was wonderful.

Lina's mother, Paulina, with husband Michael Zornick, 1953

By June we had decided to get married in August, shocking most people with the shortness of time since we had started dating. We could not see any reason for waiting once we had made the decision.

"Lina will not have enough time to get ready, dear," Andrew's mother said to us.

"All I need to get ready is my wedding dress," I replied.

As it turned out, it was just as well we gave in to pressure and made December 17 our wedding date instead, as Andrew was very ill throughout August with scarlet fever.

Andrew found a job for me at a children's home just around the corner from his home in Clothilde Street Mount Lawley, Perth. I think it is still a children's receiving home. We did not have many children stay indefinitely, though some lodged with us for six months or more. We had one deaf three-year-old boy who became my shadow. He had so much to contend with from not understanding others. One example is from mealtimes: he would be dragged into the dining room by force, then he would sit under a table and only come out once he saw other children eating. It was terrible to see his confusion.

I loved working there. After the often alarming and appalling experiences at Claremont, it was so peaceful, and this contrast struck me powerfully. During time off, I would walk to Andrew's home. I soon realised that Andrew's mother was all I ever wanted to become like if I had thought about it at all. She was very pretty, despite her age. She was 51, which was old to a 21-year-old, yet she was beautiful in every way, not just due to her physical appearance. She was extremely kind, always helpful to others and kept her house in immaculate condition. It ran like clockwork: breakfast, morning tea, lunch, afternoon tea and dinner – you could almost set your watch to the mealtimes! And yet, she was not a slave to convention. She was a warm human being who had a lot on her plate, and the only way for her to get through it all was to organise her time to fit it all in, which she did.

I turned 22 in August, when Andrew was so very sick. His mother and I thought we would lose him and his doctor did not know what was wrong. He was just burning up before our eyes. Somehow, he survived the malady. He was very weak and the skin on his hands started to peel. It was then that the doctor said that he had scarlet fever.

After he recovered, we just rolled along the road of happiness and joy. The two weeks of night duty came in very handy, as that was when I cut out the lace for my veil with nail scissors, all 15 yards or so of it. When you have no possessions other than yourself it becomes very important to look your very best. I enjoyed designing and making my own wedding gown. It was all my own creation, from start to finish. I was flying so high on love that I felt there was nothing I could not do. I constantly had Andrew's face in my mind's eye when we were apart and while cutting out the lace and sewing it. I so much wanted him to be proud of me. After all, he was marrying a foreigner, not someone of his own nationality as he should have according to tradition or 'the norm'. I did not want him to be embarrassed or feel sorry for me. I wanted to be his jewel, his treasure, his special foreigner, the love of his life.

17 December 1953 finally arrived. I was with my mother and sisters in the Kelmscott Nissan hut camp. A Russian friend volunteered to be my taxi driver. He had a beautiful Holden car. I saw him wash and polish it that morning.

I ran across to him and said, "Anatolie, be happy for me! Why do you look so sad?"

Some years later I found out why he was so despondent that day. It was the collapse of his dream, completely unknown to me at the time. After all, only a year earlier he had taught me to ice skate for a considerable length of time, but he had never indicated any romantic inclinations. I guess in hindsight he knew that if he had, I would have stopped seeing him as my feelings for him were purely platonic.

However, our journey from Kelmscott to St John's Lutheran church in Aberdeen Street told the full story. In the rear-vision mirror his feelings were written all over his face.

"Anatolie, why did you want to take me to the church feeling as you do?" I asked.

"I just wanted to be part of your wedding on any terms," he said quietly.

My sadness did not last very long, however. There was too much love and joy in my heart. How would Andrew see me as I walked down the aisle towards him? I knew I would be able to tell from his face if he felt pride and ecstasy or compassion mixed with love. I wanted the first with all my heart.

Andrew's face did tell the full story. As the *Wedding March* began, he turned his head and, on seeing me, was clearly stunned. I was delighted. It was worth all the endless hours of sewing and cutting just to please Andrew.

It was pure magic. His father married us and his mother had decorated the church, his sister and a Russian friend of mine were bridesmaids, and my five-year-old niece and nephew were flower girl and pageboy. My sisters and my mother were all full of joy.

After the ceremony, once outside, I noticed quite a few of our camp people were there just to see me get married. Some gave me gifts as I entered the taxi, and the magic of it all just continued on and on. I was very moved by the presents from these poor people, as they had so little and yet gave gifts to us.

The wedding reception was held at Chesterton Lodge in South Perth. It was a very hot day, 106 degrees by the old scale with a strong easterly wind. We also had a garden at our disposal to go out into and enjoy hearing a band play all night. I danced and danced without feeling tired. I was so high on happiness. I enjoyed every minute of my wedding day, from the time I opened my eyes before dawn until I closed them in Andrew's arms. We stayed the night at a hotel in Stirling Street and went to Andrew's place in the morning, then on to Geraldton later in the day. We stayed almost a week.

On returning in time for Christmas, we moved into a back room of Andrew's parents' house. It was just big enough for a wardrobe, a double bed and little else, but it was more than we needed. It was our little world, a world of love. Andrew's mum and dad became my mum and dad. They were so loving towards me and I did my very best to fit in with them.

Andrew's parents worked really well together. I tried to do the chores she liked least, one of which was ironing. She told me more than once that she hated ironing, so I did the lot. This was before drip-dry shirts came along, so they all had to be ironed. I had Andrew's seven shirts, his surgery gowns, bibs used on patients, tablecloths, serviettes and, of course, his father's shirts. His sister did her own ironing.

On wash days it was just Mum and I that worked through the laundry. Mum had a washing machine and a wringer. A lot of things got boiled in the copper, so that had to be lit. Mum could always tell when I started to feel tired.

"You are getting pale dear," she would say. "Go upstairs and put the kettle on."

Soon we would be having morning tea. I loved working with Andrew's mother. She always showed so much appreciation for everything I did. Dinners were really special: she cooked beautiful meals and presented them in beautiful ways, with table settings that were very pleasing.

Sundays were really special, with church in the morning, dinner at midday and then doing whatever we felt like in the afternoon.

For a time, I worked with Andrew as his dental nurse, which I liked very much. I thought life was perfect. I visited my family once a week or so. I really missed them and was afraid of moving away from them and yet, if I wanted to be a success in my new world, I had to let go of my old world, my Russian and German world. I always wanted Andrew to be proud of me, to be an asset to him, not a handicap. Of course, I had to learn English, and quickly, so I read a lot of books on early WA history, as well as novels.

Though it somehow seemed an impossibility, my two worlds had to blend. I wanted so much to have roots, to belong, to free myself of the 'displaced person' label that I had carried for seven years. I wanted to belong. Andrew's world of love and peace was what I sought. His parents stood for all things good and noble, and the love they passed on to everyone they came into contact with flowed freely all the time. Andrew's dad had the church and its many people to care for and his mum had both church and a constant flow of people to her home on all days between Sundays. She always had a ready cup of tea and something to eat at hand and spent most Fridays baking for her family and callers.

Moving to our own house was magical. We worked so hard together on so many projects: carports, pergolas, retaining walls, vegetable growing – you name it, we did it together on our little block.

About three years after we were married, I underwent my first major surgery. My mother came to stay with us to look after Andrew and the house while I was in hospital. Andrew gave Mum a terrible shock on returning from hospital. He threw himself on the bed and wept.

Mum could not speak much English, she just said, "Lina dead?"

Andrew shook his head. The following day he brought my mother to the hospital as she could not find peace until she saw for herself that I was alive. It was a long journey back to health. I would sit outside, near where Andrew worked in the garden. He built a rose garden in front of the house while I watched him huddled up in a blanket. Andrew took me to Bunbury for a five-day holiday. We stayed at the

Rose Hotel and it was wonderful. I was so confident that with all the infection cleared up, the ovarian cyst removed, I would be able to conceive and have children.

We had one more mountain to climb later, however, but this time together. In my operation I lost a fallopian tube, so my chances of conceiving were at the very least cut in half. At my final check-up with a specialist, he told me that my chances of ever conceiving were very slim. This was before in-vitro fertilisation. Today, that would be possible, but not in the 1950s.

I could not believe that I might end up childless. Children had always been part of my thinking, feelings, my whole being for as long as I can remember – certainly since my little brother had died. Now this slim chance of conceiving: no, this couldn't happen to me! Andrew could not have been more supportive and loving. If it is meant to happen, it will, we both felt, and we tried not to fret, which was pretty hard not to do for several years as most of my contemporaries were having babies – a constant reminder of what was not happening for me. I still believed strongly that I would have children, though, that this was my destiny. I just did not know how or when.

Nearly two years later, a doctor friend of ours visited us. We liked them very much and had a nice afternoon tea together.

As he was leaving, he said almost in passing, "You both sound so busy in all your ventures, so it would not really suit you to have a child right now. I have a patient who is three months pregnant. She is having the baby adopted out, but I can see the timing is not good from your point of view."

I was stunned by what he had said, and Andrew looked at me questioningly.

I looked at him and said, "What if the doctor had come to tell us I was pregnant, how would we react?"

"We would be in heaven," Andrew replied.

I said, "So, what's the difference?"

Andrew said, "None."

I ran to the phone, but Andrew said the doctor would not be home yet. We said very little while we waited for the doctor to get home. After making several calls, I finally I heard his voice on the other end the line.

I said, "Yes, John, this is a child for us."

This was how our number one came into being and became part of us.

Lina and Andrew on their wedding day.

Chapter 10 – Children

I trace my obsession with children to a part of my life when I was age 11 and spent four months with my one-year-old brother, each of us depending on the other for our survival. Less than a year later he had died before our eyes from lack of nourishment.

I have always felt that my life would be with children. When I was told in young adulthood that my chances of conceiving were slim, the shock lasted only a short while. I knew I would have children; I just did not know how or when.

When the opportunity to adopt arrived, I thought a lot about the young woman who carried the child and wished she could have been part of my joy, but it did not seem feasible to make her part of our family as anything but the child's mother and it all came unstuck. No, there was no way other than for her to decide what was best for the child and for me to do likewise and not look back until the child was no longer a youngster, and only then to encourage the tracing of genetic roots if he or she was interested.

When children came my way, I saw them as a gift from God. My first adoption came in such a natural way that, for seven months, I did what any expectant mother does, prepare. I sewed lots of clothes, lined a pram with nice material of a neutral colour as I did not know if the baby was going to be a boy or a girl. I ran to my neighbour, Mrs Dawson, to show her what I had made, seeking her advice on the size of garments, but I basically just wanted to share my joy with someone while Andrew was at work and my mother and sisters too far away to walk to.

As time went on, I spent more and more time with my mother and sisters. The last few weeks were the slowest and I spent the final week with my family, to be within easy reach of them when the time came to receive the infant. They lived in Queens Park which is close to Victoria Park, where the child was to be born in a small hospital.

The baby was born at 5.15am. Andrew was shaving when the phone rang. It was the doctor, ringing from the hospital to announce the arrival of our first born, a baby boy. We were so excited we did not know what to do with ourselves. On his way to work, Andrew dropped me off at my sister Irma's place. My sisters lived next door to each other and Mother in the next street, so we were all pretty much together. By then, both my sisters had two children each – both had a 10-year-old and a two-year-old and had had to work, as well as their husbands, to be able to save for a house. This was the reason for the big gap between their children's ages.

Our joy and excitement knew no bounds. We could not wait until the telephone call came to say that we could come and pick the baby up. This was not until the eighth day after birth. I drove Andrew to work, then drove to my sisters' places to pick them up and be on our way. I was finally going to pick up my baby, and I would never be childless again. I, too, would now be like my sisters and most of my contemporaries. A beautiful new world awaited.

We were kept waiting at the hospital, The matron was very abrupt and slow in completing the procedures. I was puzzled and, eventually, asked the matron if I was doing anything wrong.

She looked up from her papers and said, "No, of course not. It is just that the girl had a very hard time giving birth and you are taking the baby. I got too emotionally involved with her."

I just looked at her, waiting for her to make the next move. She apologised and tried to be nice.

As I remember it

"Matron, I had nothing to do with her decision, did I?" I asked:

She was really nice after that. I asked if there was anything I could do to help the girl and the matron said, "She could do without the hospital bill."

I agreed, but it was a bit of a dampener and I felt it was a bit unfair on me. I truly felt sorry for the girl who, for reasons of her own, had decided to walk away from the child she had carried and given birth to. In my heart, I had always known I could never do such a thing, but then, I had my mother and sisters to support me. If the mother of this child was on her own, but with the social security we have now, it may have been a different story.

All this sadness only lasted until I held the little boy, Richard, in my arms. My middle sister, Irma, was with me. She was furious with the matron, but I understood the dilemma she was in. Whichever way you looked at it, you could not get away from the sad side of the situation.

My first child was followed by son number two and, six years later, by number three, our daughter. The excitement and joy I experienced with receiving and raising each child, the awe, the wonder of it all, simply being a part of the arrival of new life on this planet and taking care of it, were immense.

A week to 10 days is a long time to wait for a newborn straight after the trauma of birth, but that was how the system worked. I did not see the babies until one week to 10 days later. I can still see my second son's angry little face as he looked at me for the first time. Once I held him to my heart, I refused to put him down, even though I was meant to come back the following day to pick him up. The matron at Ngala Hospital in Kensington, WA, was a special person: she decoded what she saw and I took the baby home.

I have always felt great love and compassion for the women who carried my children, but newborns can only handle one set of parents, therefore, later in life when they are no longer children, they should have the opportunity to meet their genetic mothers and fathers but on the level of genetic relations not as another set of parents. It is not fair on the child to do it any other way. As far as I understand and have experienced, and for reasons we may never fully understand, this is how it was for us: one gives up the child, the other nurtures the child she did not carry.

In our youth, we are very good at putting aside the things we cannot alter, but it is quite a different story once we have lived and experienced a lot in life. Anyway, once I was home with my mother and sisters, the joy of this little life swept me along so forcibly that there was no room for anything else. I received the same welcome I was part of when my sisters came home with their new babies. My mother unwrapped him and kissed his little hands and feet.

"To think that people say there are no miracles when we are surrounded by the wonder of creation, and the biggest of them all is a human life. Look how perfect he is," she said as she held him gently to her heart.

I wondered if she was thinking of the little boy we had lost, but neither of us put our thoughts into words. This was a day of joy, no room for sadness, no room for clouds to dampen our spirits.

The next six months just flew by, going from joy to joy. I was concerned about my baby not getting the ideal nutrition: breast milk. I added vitamins to his milk and basically let him be the judge of how much and when he ate. Andrew was a great help, telling me to trust my instincts and his judgement. I know this sounds ridiculous, but it worked, and our baby grew from strength to strength. Both our doctor friend who had delivered him and the clinic sister were full of praise. Everything they said was very confidence-building for any new mum.

My mother was diagnosed with a shadow on her lungs and was isolated for six months. We had Maria living with Andrew and I, Maria whom I took out of Claremont Mental Hospital after she had spent seven years as a patient there. There were many reasons for her state, one of which was leaving her three-year-old son behind in Poland when she and her husband ran for their lives in 1945. She never got over it, going from breakdown to breakdown until she ended up in Claremont, a life sentence it seemed. I had worked with Maria in Mt Henry in my early years in Australia, but had lost track of her as our paths went in different directions.

Seven years later I found out her whereabouts. I was shocked to find that she had been in the asylum all those years. She was unrecognisable, almost black from seven years of summer sunshine. She would sit outside and not move into shade unless someone moved her. She must have been forgotten by staff when on the wrong side of the shade and copped the full blast of the summer sun to make her this black.

I had never seen my mother so unreasonably frightened, but the spectre of mental illness had this effect on her. She was alarmed beyond reason and asked me to take Maria back to hospital before she killed or maimed us, especially the nine-month-old baby.

"You can't expose him to such danger, the unknown," she said. "The mental asylum and all. The baby is defenceless, you must protect him."

For the first time in my life, I could not do what Mother asked of me. To return Maria to the asylum at that point would have been a life sentence and I could not do that to her, or anyone else for that matter. I knew what Claremont was like, having worked there. It was inhumane in my eyes. And besides, Maria was convinced that her state was incurable. It was I who kept saying to her it was completely up to her. I promised Mum I would find a supported flat for her that would make us all safe, although at the time I had no idea how this could happen. Eventually we found a supported flat which was associated with the Claremont Mental Hospital and arranged for her to spend some time there.

At first, Maria hated being separated from all her loved ones, especially thanks to her limited knowledge of English. However, she adjusted, just as she did with all her other experiences, unacceptable as they often were. We all visited her as often as we could, which was frequently. She even made friends with inmates and staff during the six months of her stay back in Claremont.

Maria made good progress on her road to recovery. All I did was tell her it was completely up to her which way she went, either back to Claremont or back to life and she believed me and finished up making a complete recovery. The old doctor, Dr Teaberg, the head of psychiatry at Claremont at that time was overjoyed with Maria's improvement. Like Maria, he was also from Poland and knew what had brought her to breaking point. He had tried very hard to help her when she was admitted to the hospital.

"Doctor, what are you saving me for?" she would ask him. "To be sane in a mental asylum knowing I will never get out of here? No, I'd sooner die."

She tried to starve herself to death but was forced to eat: she was not allowed to die.

Dr Teaberg told me that in all his experience with mental illness he had never come across someone like Maria, who one day divorced herself from herself and completely shut herself off from reality. A lot of patients did this, but not to the same degree as Maria had for seven long years. To see her return to life was miraculous, not only in my eyes but also in Dr Teaberg's.

Maria's recovery also meant the beginning of her search for her son, who by now was 17. She went to the immigration department and the Red Cross. She knocked on as many doors as was necessary to achieve her goal, and achieve it she did. It was very difficult to get anyone out of communist-occupied countries, let alone a young male of military age. We are speaking of the early 1960s when there were very strict laws to stop people from leaving the 'iron curtain'.

Dr Teaberg helped her to get a job as a nursing aide at the Home of Peace. She was so compassionate towards all who suffered. This was only six months from the time she left Claremont – her job and how great she was with it really seemed like a miracle. Maria had been a beautician, so she knew what to do to bring her skin back to its usual condition, and she had her hair styled. After all, she was only 37, but she looked like a much older woman.

This was another thing she could not adjust to, being seven years older. She felt she hadn't lived for seven years, and had no recollection of the passing of all that time. But she would comfort herself by saying to me that I, too, was seven years older now.

"Yes, Maria, I am," I would reply. "I am 27 now, no longer 20 as I was when you knew me before you lost your seven years. We are both seven years older."

"Thirty-seven," she would say. "Where have I been those last seven years?"

Andrew lost his offsider, for the outdoor projects anyway. However, most of our back and front yards were full of all sorts of projects. After all, we had been working on them for three years. How much can you fit into a little block in Mt Lawley, which was less than a quarter of an acre? Little did I know that Andrew had dreams of having land to work on and enjoy. A small suburban block does not give you that opportunity.

It began with our Sunday afternoon drives in the hills. Up Kalamunda Road with all the beautiful houses and gardens, magnificent trees, tree ferns and more.

In those days, Lesmurdie was country. Although it was close to Perth, it was wonderfully rural and quiet. We found three acres of land set back from Welshpool Road in Lesmurdie. We sold our house and lived with my mother while our new house was being built. Our three-acre-property in Lesmurdie was an old citrus orchard. We proceeded to plant trees as our house was being built.

Later, we moved into a flat in South Perth: at Mill Point Road, not far from the river. We enjoyed our stay in our flat there. Every night after tea we went for little walks with our son.

Maria continued to live with us until she remarried, after being a widow for about nine years. She asked our advice as to what to do, but how can you advise on something so personal? She took the plunge and married the wrong man as things turned out. She got her son out of Poland only to be attacked by a bitter 18-year-old, angry with her for having left him. She had no defence. His father was dead, so the son put all the blame for his abandonment on Maria. She gave birth to another son, but it did nothing to heal the marriage or her first son's attitude. It was very, very sad to stand by and not be able to change things for the better. It took her first son 11 years to learn the truth of how it had all happened, that his parents had fled communism and probably certain death. It was during one of Maria's many subsequent breakdowns that I asked him for his help. At first, he said that he did not want to help his mother, but he could see the strain it was putting on me. It was then that he found out what had really happened, and he forgave his mother.

We moved into our house in Lesmurdie in 1960. We planted so many trees we lost count. All along Gladys Road, the lemon-scented spotted gums and Tasmanian blue gums are enormous now. We also grew lots of vegetables and had a little orchard, with a large range of fruit trees. A certain section of the block had to be drained, so Andrew dug trench after trench, filled them with blue metal and achieved a beautiful result. We had a creek running through our property and were never short of water. We had a beautiful tropical section just outside a large window. A Siberian elm was at the centre of this section, and all around it were Monstera deliciosas, philodendrons, azaleas and heaps of ferns. It was just stunning. I loved that house and the land it was on. I was truly happy and at peace. If it was not for the events that happened much later, we would never have left it.

Our next joy was David. The matron from Ngala rang Andrew, whom she knew from when he had been tutoring her mother-craft nurses. She asked if we were interested in adding to our family. She had a little one there and she could recommend us as suitable parents. Once again, we were delighted. Without any hesitation we felt he was for us. A week later, I became a mother for the second time.

My children have always known that I did not carry them, that they were adopted. That's what adoption meant to me and my children. I did not carry them, that was all, but in every sense they were mine, as much as any child could be. No one owns anyone, and also this applies to other parents. None of us belong completely to another being. Children are lent to us, to take care of, to teach and love, and they in turn will generally do the same for their children: this is the cycle of love and life.

When my children were little, they wanted to know how I found them. Each of them had a story of their arrival and my part in it. Richard, my first, I could tell a lot: how I waited for seven months, how his dad was shaving when the doctor rang at 5:15 in the morning and cut himself. How excited we were.

David, our second son, had a nice story, too.

He used to say to me, "How did you know it was me, Mum?"

"I did not know at all," I would reply. "All I saw was a long-legged baby with beautiful hands who had his eyes closed, and then he opened his eyes and looked at me with such determination, as much as to say, 'Where have you been for a whole week? I have been here for a whole week, Mum', and I instantly knew it was you, David."

Natasha, our third, was a Goldfields baby, not that she was born there, but we lived there at the time of her birth. It was the matron of Ngala Mother and Child Centre who said she knew immediately she saw Natasha that she was a baby for us. When Andrew made contact with her, she said she had been waiting for us to contact her and the story went on from there.

The children all enjoyed their little stories. Being adopted or, rather, not being genetically ours, did not surface until they were in late primary school when they became aware of the absence of a genetic link between us. A lot of it was the result of other children's curiosity.

"What is it like to be adopted?" they would ask.

This would annoy David enormously, and he would say to them, "What is it like not to be adopted? It's a silly question." He would end the conversation that way.

We were all very comfortable with our situation because we were so happy. I often spoke to Andrew of how nice it would be if we could incorporate our children's natural parents into our family but, after closer consideration, we felt the risk of our children becoming confused about their identity was too great. We decided that the most important thing was to bring the children up with love and security. The rest could be tackled when they grew up and could make their own decisions, which I would wholly support.

We were a very happy family. Every school holiday we took the children either to Rottnest Island or to sheep stations such as Kanandah, Maron, to name a few, also to Narrogin and the Lange family. For 11 years, we rented a cottage at Rottnest Island and loved it. When the boys were old enough to enjoy fishing, Andrew would hire a boat and go out on the water with them while I stayed on the beach. Natasha, too, used to go with them. It gave me a chance to get tea ready and to read. I read a lot – usually I got through a book the size of James Mitchener's *The Source* (about 1100 pages) while at Rottnest.

I loved sitting on the beach at dusk. I love the beach at all times, but the quietness of sunset was special and magical. On Andrew and the children's return, we would have a bagful of herrings to descale and clean, but the joy on the boys' and Natasha's faces made it all worthwhile. Andrew loved fish so much he could eat it just on its own, whereas I need a lot of trimmings with it and still only manage to eat a small portion at the most. The children also only ate small amounts of the fish, but loved catching them. Bike riding was another joy at Rottnest Island. There were no cars, just people and bikes. Even when they were little and on their first two-wheelers, we felt safe in allowing the children ride on their own.

I also loved walking on the edge of the water all the way to the natural jetty. On the walk I would go past the army barracks to where the calm waters of the bay met the southerly side of the island, where strong winds and waves were usually very evident. It was beautiful. So quiet. It seemed too far for most people to walk, so it was mainly free of them. You could sunbathe and swim naked, and we did. It was completely private. Well, if someone did venture that far, which was a rarity, we could see them coming long before they could see us.

Going to the sheep stations in winter was another highlight of our younger lives. We came in contact with Kanandah sheep station, east of Kalgoorlie, when we lived in Kalgoorlie. Andrew was working at Boulder Dental Clinic and was the flying dentist for all the surrounding areas. He would travel with the flying doctor on regular clinic trips. He was treating patients on Kanandah one Friday and was invited to stay the weekend as they had a gymkhana on that weekend. The doctor's wife and I received telegrams telling us to be on such and such train and to get off at Naretha railway siding.

Naretha is 200 miles from Kalgoorlie. We had no idea what was there, and the doctor's wife and I had never met. Well, I trusted Andrew implicitly. I picked up six-month-old Natasha, dressed three-year-old David and Richard, who was nearly five, dressed himself and we went to the railway station. The passengers on the train seemed intrigued by us. Two women, six children, two of them babies, who were apparently going to disembark in the middle of a desert.

After many hours of travelling, we arrived at Naretha, which consisted of four posts and a piece of corrugated iron, and that was all. The train stopped, but the passengers refused to let us off the train until they saw a four-wheel-drive vehicle approaching in the distance. They waited a little longer until they could see the face of the driver. We disembarked, very grateful to the passengers. I was a little frightened and, with a baby in my arms and two little ones by my side, was feeling very vulnerable. The passengers waved and the train driver tooted as we were greeted by our hostess. It was the station manager's wife, Ruth, who greeted us. That was the beginning of a lifetime friendship between us and the Swanns.

The gymkhana was very different from anything that I had experienced in my life. People rode on their horses for days just to be there. The men looked as if they were from Western films and seemed to be as one with their horses. Breakfast was early, a barbecue, with open fires and lots of boiling billies: cups of tea simply flowed. After breakfast, there was the long ride to the site of the races. I noticed some of the horsemen sniggering as they looked at Andrew – a city slicker, they thought. I knew that Andrew had been a pretty good horseman in his youth, as I had heard lots of stories about those days. I walked up to Andrew and asked him to show those men that he could hold his own despite being from the city. He said he was sure he could handle a horse, despite the length of time since he had been on one.

"You just show them," I said.

He smiled and replied, "Do you really want me to ride?"

"Yes."

He then borrowed someone's jeans. Word got around that the dentist thought he could ride a horse, so the men were going to teach him a lesson by giving him what seemed a rather 'difficult' horse. They laughed as the animal tried to throw Andrew off, but their amusement soon stopped when he got the horse under control and rode off with the rest of them to the race site.

He even entered one or two events before he rode up to me and said, "Will this do?"

"Yes, thank you," I said.

We had a wonderful day. The boys loved it, but they had to be watched closely as they were so little among all the big men and horses.

We did not move to Kalgoorlie by choice, but from necessity. Andrew had developed terrible asthma and he was not responding to any treatment, including drugs. We discovered that dry climate agreed with his condition and Kalgoorlie was very dry and hot for more than half of the year. So, we picked up our little family and moved there.

Before going to Kalgoorlie, we had tried sea air. We went to Busselton and a lot of other coastal places, but while we loved Busselton, we found out after a while that Andrew's asthma flared up worse than ever. He had committed himself to running the practice as a locum while the other dentist went on holidays. From the first day of our second trip to Busselton his asthma worsened. He struggled through the five days of work.

Many times ensued when I thought Andrew would not make it through the night, and I still don't know how he did. On Friday evenings he would drive to Narrogin in order to breathe. We knew that dry air agreed with his health and, yes, he did get relief while he was there. We were very fortunate to have a friend on a farm just half an hour's drive out of Narrogin. This was another beautiful family, the Langes. Andrew had known them from his early youth. When he was a student, he had spent many holidays on their father's farm. The owner at the time my husband went there for clean air was Geoff, who was a little older than Andrew. They became the best of friends.

So, the Langes' place was Andrew's second home. I was so glad he could go somewhere where he could not only breathe but be with people whom he loved and who loved him in return.

Andrew had found an employment opportunity in the Kalgoorlie area quickly enough. A dentist was needed in Boulder, so Andrew accepted the job. We packed our few belongings and, with the caravan in tow, went to Kalgoorlie. It seemed like the end of the world, but just the thought of Andrew being able to breathe put all else on hold. On arrival, we were shown the house set aside for the dentist. It was terribly run down. You could look outside through the cracks and creatures could slip in and out of the place. It got very hot inside. The authorities assured us that it would be repaired as soon as possible, but when, no one could tell. It is amazing what one can adjust to when there is no choice. Andrew and I talked: we had two choices – make the most of it or be miserable. We decided to make the most of it.

We had 16-year-old Carole with us – she had joined our family almost a year earlier and went back to school when Andrew's asthma got out of control. We had taken her under our wing to give her a better quality of life, and here we were with a mountain of our own to climb. However, she fitted in very well and continued her education. We focused on being happy and on doing as much for others as we could.

It began with Carole, then Andrew's nephew Ian joined us. He was working as a radio announcer and was 19 years old at the time. Pastor Klein also used to come every second or third week to stay with us. When he came to visit, a whole lot of other people came with him. He gathered people from all over the Goldfields and some of them ended up at our place.

Before we took the drastic step of moving to a new home, Andrew had met a woman who was 30 years ahead of her time in terms of asthma treatment. She advocated then what is being advocated now, but three decades ago she encountered a wall of opposition from the professionals at that time. What she said made perfect sense to Andrew, but his asthma was so far advanced that it needed more care and action than what she recommended. He needed to be where he could breathe and then follow her instructions. So, every time we came to Perth, he looked her up. The remedy was simple enough: no drugs, and breathing exercises every morning without fail. He followed her instructions to the letter. Every time he did it right, he got an asthma attack and would be gasping for breath but. At the same time, however, he brought up phlegm that cleared his lungs and gave him a chance of ridding himself of asthma altogether once his lungs were cleared of the accumulated fluid. It was wonderful to know that there was a cure and most of it was up to him, with no drug dependency.

The other thing he did was ride a bicycle to work from Bourke Street in Kalgoorlie to Boulder Clinic. In Kalgoorlie, there were no underground pipes to take rainwater away, but there were dips at every crossroads. You went down one side and up the other. So, all the way it was up and down rather than flat. This made it a lot more strenuous, but Andrew persevered and rid himself of asthma. As he played squash as well, he also got very fit.

As mentioned, it was Matron Grant from Ngala who recommended Natasha, our third child, to us. It was quite remarkable for the matron to be so sure that this baby was for us. With joy in our hearts, we all came to Perth and stayed with my mother, who was delighted to have us. My stepfather, Deda also loved our boys. Andrew went for his appointment and I went to Ngala and my little daughter. My mother and sisters once again awaited us. The baby was welcomed with so much love, and the boys were delighted at this little bundle of magic, Natasha. Before returning to Kalgoorlie, we saw Andrew's parents, who were just as delighted.

One other special thing occurred while we were in Kalgoorlie. I received a visit from a repertory theatre director, who invited me to join it. I was delighted. I had a little experience in acting and a lot more in dancing, but I had not done either since I married.

"Why not?" Andrew said. "Do whatever you like,"

So, I did. The first year I had leading parts in four plays, the second year, six. It was so exciting, and I loved acting. One play was called *Bonaventure*, or *Thunder On The Hill* as a film based upon the play was called. It was a three-act play. I played the part of a mother superior: it was a 'nun fiction'. The play ran for three weeks and was wonderful.

Another play which had a profound impact on me was a drama in which I played the part of a young mother whose six-year-old child was missing and later found drowned. My voice was recorded in a makeshift echo chamber and presented as my thoughts on being told that my child had drowned, which was most effective. As you can well imagine, it was a heavy drama and it left quite an impression on audiences.

From left, David, Andrew, Richard, Lina and Natasha, in Kalgoorlie.

Chapter 11 – After Kalgoorlie

I think the 10 or more years after returning from Kalgoorlie were the happiest of my life, if it is possible at all to pick such a period. Perhaps 'the most exciting and interesting' is a more appropriate statement. So many doors opened for me that had previously seemed shut. My children were at their closest to me at that stage of their lives and I loved it. The boys brought an endless string of friends with them from school, most of them just followed each of them home and I fed and watered them all. They had such fun on our three acres. They had a cricket pitch and more, and I made pilmenje[11] for them all, even taught some of them how to prep and cook it. I meet adults now who remember the fun they had as kids at our place, and, of course, the pilmenje story.

I started keep-fit classes in the large family room at the end of our house and also taught lessons at school, teaching children movement to music and Russian dance.

We became a branch of the Save The Children Fund and began fundraising events. One stands out vividly because it was held at our place. We had suckling pig on a spit, a dance floor and a band. It turned out to be a very special night. The grounds looked beautiful, all lit up, and we were all dressed glamorously. It was a magical night and lots of money was raised. We donated all the food and, of course, all our effort and time, so most of the money for the tickets went to the Save The Children Fund. Oh yes, halfway through the night the dance floor collapsed. Andrew crawled underneath to fix it and a beautiful woman followed him to help.

---

[11] Pilmenje are meat-filled dumplings, a traditional Russian food.

On seeing this, my sister Irma promptly followed, grabbed the woman by an ankle and pulled her out from underneath the dance floor, saying: "He is my sister's husband, get out of there."

The poor woman sat on the grass, shaking her head. "I was only trying to help." she said.

"Oh, yes?" my sister replied.

It caused quite some entertainment which I had missed by running around, being the hostess. I missed my sister's performance.

I studied piano-accordion at that time, too, and enjoyed it immensely. I could go on and on itemising the joys of my life back then. So many challenges, and so many exciting things that I was part of.

Sister Kate's children's home was another beautiful part of my life at that time. Rhonda, the matron at that time brought a little busful of children to our place once a week to do dance and exercise to music. It was such a beautiful experience. The children, Rhonda and I all had a wonderful time. These afternoons lasted for more than a decade, until 1974 to be exact.

Nineteen Sixty-Nine was both a beautiful and tragic year. My mother had a heart attack, her second and not long after the first. A doctor told us the next one could be fatal. My eldest sister, Lucya, sold her house in Cannington and bought a block of land just up the road from us, in Brady Road, while we lived in Marri Crescent. She quickly organised for a duplex to be built so that Mother could be within earshot.

My mother and stepfather, Deda, sold their house to pool their resources. Deda went to live with my middle sister, Irma, while Mum came to stay with us. It was wonderful. The boys were at school, Natasha was still at home and would turn five in September that same year. I went to work for Andrew for a while as Mum stayed home with Natasha and the boys after school.

Lucya and her family moved in with their Russian friends. This turned out to be disastrous as both the husband and wife were alcoholics. When under the influence of liquor, they became quite violent towards each other. It terrified Lucya's children. She comforted them, of course, but could focus on one thing only, Mum, and getting her back to her old self. She borrowed more money and furnished the flat, even including carpets – Mum had to have the best, she reasoned. Lucya worked for more than a decade to pay off the debt, as well getting her children educated.

Meanwhile, Mum's stay with us was very special, as her close relationship with us all increased immensely, particularly with our children and Andrew. My children remember her as the quietly spoken Oma (grandmother) who left not a shadow of doubt as to her unconditional love for them.

As time went by, she became more and more silent. However, once Andrew was at work and the children at school, she overflowed with feelings, largely concerning her tragic past. They seemed to overpower her and she could only talk about her pain, *Galadovka*, my father's destruction, my little brother's suffering and death. We both relived it all and wept. I tried to point out to her how destructive all this was, both to her and myself, and I pleaded with her to look ahead.

"Focus on now, Mum, on your triumphs, on all the love seeds you have planted and how they are thriving," I said. "You are loved so much by so many."

I told her I didn't want to go back to the places where evil had reigned and almost swallowed us up. What was the point of going through this pain all over again?

Her eyes would fill with tears as she said, "But, darling, this is all I feel."

"We have to move beyond it, Mum," I replied. "We have to move to now, to love, to peace. Please, Mum, shut the door on our past or it will rob us of our present."

We see things so clearly when we are young. Looking back now, I feel I did not understand her, I just wanted to run away from it all and take Mum with me. I was 37 and had been in Australia for less than 20 years. I wanted to nurture my peaceful roots, which were very shallow indeed. Seeing Mum could take me back to the 'other' self so easily. I was determined not to let my past rob me of what I had found and nurtured with all my heart. No, I would not let go of love and peace.

It took at least 20 years of living and learning for me to understand my mother. I certainly did not at the time, but I knew that she understood me. She always had. It is easy to be wise in hindsight.

I watched Lucya and Mum very closely, but they seemed to be on a different wavelength to me. The non-verbal connection between them was so powerful and, as I saw no opportunity to be part of it, I just kept myself busy, fitting more and more into each day, keeping in close touch with them but only on the perimeters of their experience. Mum and Lucya moved into their duplex homes only months before my mother's final heart attack. She was rushed to Bentley Hospital, never to regain consciousness. My sisters and I kept up our vigil. One of us was always by her side. We wanted to be there should she come to. I took some crocheting with me, as doing something with my hands helped to pass the time.

Irma lived just two doors down the road from us. It was so easy for the children to walk down the hill to Aunty Irma, and her TV, of course: we still didn't have one. Mum, too, walked to Irma's place, comfortably but slowly behind the children, whom she loved being with. I had a Mrs Edward coming in twice a week to clean and do a wash if I needed. She became part of our family, another grandmother, and she was a wonderful person. Our children still remember her fondly. Mum did not have to do any housework, only what she felt like doing, if anything, but she always cooked beautiful evening meals that were ready for serving by the time Andrew and I came home from work. It was so wonderful to enter the house welcomed by the smell of delicious food.

I did not work with Andrew for long. I missed the children and also wanted to spend more time with my mother. In my heart I knew she would not last long, but, when the final heart attack occurred, it shattered me to the very core. People like her don't just die! They are such an integral part of life and love, of all that is worth living for ... how can they die and disappear from this earth? Complete disbelief set in and stopped the healing process completely. I guess I was in denial.

Mother used to sit in on my exercise sessions. She would not speak, but just sit, all peaceful and serene. She projected wordless love to all. I wished she would take her apron off — this seemed so un-Australian. I did not want her to look like a foreigner. How selfish I must have been to mind a little thing like that, but I wanted her to be a part of the Australian part of me, not the unusual or different parts.

I felt very bad about this when she died. How could I have felt anything other than joy and pride in her? I think I wanted my friends to see the part of her that I knew, which, of course, was impossible without a shared language. After my mother's death, I found out that my friends had picked up far more about who this silent person was than I ever realised. She had projected who she was without words. I must have seemed a lot more foreign than I realised, despite my Australian husband and children and my seeming security. I really did feel a strong sense of belonging, but I wanted my Australian friends to know her as she really was, not the way she seemed, a withdrawn stranger.

My mother's passing from this life had a far greater, far deeper effect on me than I would ever have imagined. Together with my sisters, we had functioned as one unit since I was five, my mother always at the centre, quietly binding us together. I was quite unprepared for the depth of pain her passing away caused.

As noted, after her third heart attack she never regained consciousness. I sat by her bed in the hope that she would recover, but we all realised this would not happen although we hoped to be able to say goodbye to her. My sisters and I took turns sitting by her bed until her heart eventually stopped beating.

Lucya would only focus on one thing and one thing alone: Mum. She would break down and weep, and then wait for Mum to open her eyes. I began to fear for Lucya. Irma and I seemed to have a better perspective. Lucya just followed her heart, which was broken. She and Mum had always had such strong hold on each other, one borne out of great suffering and joy. Lucya refused to let go of Mum. She hung onto hope for Mother's recovery with such tenacity it was frightening.

The unthinkable, the unbelievable had happened. Mum was gone and we were left behind. She was only 63, yet she had said all along how good it was to have escaped the then Russian system and the killer in the Kremlin where she was sure she would never have seen her 40th birthday, so, in that sense, she had lived a long life.

I floated in and out of different states and then engaged in as many activities as time would allow, moving as fast as I could – distracting myself in the hope of healing taking place.

My children had been very close to my mother, as were my sisters' children. This was how it came to be that my children's first language was German.

Mother had asked Andrew's permission for that and had said to him, "I don't want my grandchildren to think they had a strange grandmother who could not speak their tongue."

Andrew was delighted and began to study the German language. He kept up with Richard until he was age of two-and-a-half and began to speak fluently, leaving his dad behind: until then, we had both addressed him in German. David, our second child, picked up more English from his brother than German from us, yet, with my mother, he conversed in German. Natasha, too, conversed in German with my mother, but in English with her brothers and friends. They got a good foundation in the second language, but were too young to retain it after my mother died and the necessity of speaking it was gone. I continued to speak German to them, but they answered in English, so I let it go. I did not want them to have identity crises, I wanted them to identify as Australians.

As I sat by my mother's side, I looked at her face. Since I was five years old, I had not seen such beauty and peace on that beautiful face. This was how I remembered her from my early childhood, but I had not seen it since. This filled me with tremendous joy and peace. Wherever Mum was, I felt strongly that she was happy. Our vigil lasted until she took her last breath. It was hard to take her leaving us without saying goodbye, yet she was gone and we were left without her. It was very bewildering.

Our heads told us this was the circle of life, but our hearts did not want to hear about any of this. Our Pastor at the time, Pastor Jordan, conducted the funeral service. The only clear memory I have of the funeral is standing by Mum's coffin, looking at her gentle face and wondering how on earth I would continue my journey through life without her.

I heard firm, strong footsteps approaching from a distance. As they came closer, I recognised them as being those of Andrew's mother. She stopped by my side and, without looking around, I felt her presence and strength penetrating me. I felt I would make it, I wanted to be strong like her. She became my anchor to reality.

Life does go on despite we humans passing through it and moving into history. Once again, I threw myself into action. Distraction does help and, eventually, despite the pain, we do heal. It was harder for Lucya, whose whole world seemed to collapse around her with Mum's death. The duplex house became pointless, the debt enormous. Our stepfather brought home a woman from England whom he knew before marrying Mum, and old wounds were torn open. Lucya found the strength to try and make her welcome, even though the time for grieving was very short. The woman put pressure on Deda to break away from Lucya and her family and eventually he gave in.

Lucya and her husband Bill had to sell the duplex, which had been built originally with the help of Irma's husband, in order to repay him his share of the cost. They lost a lot of money and had to start again with another house and even bigger debts. When her youngest child went to school, Lucya went to work, full-time. My sister Irma fared better, as her husband managed to buy a front-end loader, completely on borrowed money, paid it off and finished up on a good income. He had to work extremely hard, but felt he was rewarded and provided well for his family.

A lot of things happened in 1974. I had a back injury and was having chiropractic treatment. I also met a woman who was dying from cancer while going to the clinic. Her name was Virginia and she was Swiss, and she was being treated on the tornado machine. I was asked to go and visit her as she spoke no English and I spoke German. I saw her through the last three months of her life. I took her back to Switzerland to her family and stayed with her until she died. For the last four weeks of her life, I slept in her room by her bed.

After two weeks in her room, I saw very clearly that I was losing my sense of perspective. I had nothing to hold onto except the love of a beautiful dying person, and all else became irrelevant. I told Virginia this and she understood that I had to go. However, she pleaded with me not to go straight to home Australia but to have a long stopover in London and she would try to die without me being around.

I could not refuse her. I gave her the address of where I would be staying, with a family I knew in Tunbridge Wells who said they would take me in. I had been there for a week when a telephone call came through from Virginia asking me to come back to Switzerland.

My friend Judy refused to advise me. She simply said, "Some decisions we have to make completely on our own," and she was right.

In my heart I knew there was only one way for me to complete what I had started, so I flew back the same day. If I needed a reward, the look on her face when she saw me entering the room was more than enough. I talked with her about the need for me to have a hold on reality outside her room. She agreed, but it was just a matter of days and nights for me to get back to where I was when I realised that I needed to get away. I was drawn into a kind of suffering no human being should be subjected to. I had become her vessel, her sanity, her hold on a life she had lost many months ago. Virginia refused to die, and as long as I was with her she did not.

I lost my balance in regard to the wholeness of life. Virginia's suffering was so immense that no number of drugs could relieve it. In the depth of the night when all pain is magnified, hers was beyond description, yet she told me that as long as my arm was stretched across her body, she felt no pain. I would sit like that for most of the night, until my head eventually collapsed onto her bed and she signalled for me to lie down. Semi-conscious, I would drop onto the makeshift bed and lie beside her. Her voice was barely audible, and only with an ear to her lips could I understand some of her speech. We mostly communicated with signs. Two more weeks passed without any change in Virginia's condition, or mine. I could no longer think beyond easing my friend's plight.

At the end of the second week, I went to Zurich to pick up mail from home. Andrew was deeply concerned about my wellbeing, but did not know what action to take any more than I did. It was while I was in Zurich that I was notified of Virginia's death. By the time I got back to Arlesheim in Switzerland, she was gone, and they would not let me see her. I felt that this was most unfair to both of us. She had wanted me with her when she took her last breath and I had wanted to be there. We were both cheated.

I stayed at a local hotel until her funeral. There were so many weeping people at the funeral trying to justify their absence when she needed them most. It was a stranger from Australia who did what they should have done. I was so depleted and burnt out that I could not even comfort them. I listened in silence and, when they finished, I moved on.

Standing by Virginia's grave, watching her coffin being lowered into the ground, I had a strange feeling that part of me was going with her. After the funeral I picked up my suitcase and caught a train to Zurich. I went to her ex-husband and daughter's apartment, to make my flight reservation. The apartment was full of tipsy people. They got a terrible shock at seeing me and told me there was no room for me to sleep there. I pleaded with them to put me up, anywhere at all, in the corridor, just please, please, not to put me out on the street! I felt too weak to go anywhere. I promised them I would go the next morning.

That next morning, a neighbour rang. She was a friend of Virginia's and asked me to breakfast. I was delighted to be with just one person, not surrounded by a group of grieving and resentful people. I could see the guilt they were feeling at having let Virginia down and I, a stranger, reminded them of this. It was written all over their faces. My suitcase was left outside the door with a note saying, "We are sorry, but this is the only way." I was shattered by their action. I tried very hard to focus on Andrew and the kids, but they kept disappearing, out of reach.

It was a very stressful and demanding journey, but I made it home. What I did not realise was to what degree this experience had changed me. I wanted so much for someone to understand and share my experience, starting with Andrew. I did not realise that some occurrences, those of great depth, cannot be shared: it is a solo journey. Andrew was also very tired and depleted from looking after the children while holding a full-time job for the five weeks I was away. Each of us needed comforting.

Six weeks later I was diagnosed with a growth inside me the size of a cricket ball, to use the doctor's words. In January 1975, I was admitted to a small hospital and 48 hours later I had bowel paralysis. I lost a tremendous amount of weight, and my tummy was bloated enormously. I was climbing the walls with the pain I was experiencing. There was no treatment. My gynaecologist deserted me, not even giving me an explanation as to what was happening to me.

All I could see through the haze of pain was myself having become like Virginia. How was that possible? When the bowel paralysis set in, I needed more surgery, but it didn't happen. I should have been monitored more closely after the operation, but by the time they realised the seriousness of my condition, I was too weak to go under anaesthetic. This I only found out later. At the time, I was not only fighting for my life but also my sanity. After two-and-a-half weeks, Andrew saw that there was no treatment for me at that hospital. It would be just a matter of time before I burned myself out in pain, so he took me home, to die, so it seemed to me.

January 1975 seemed to a particularly hot summer to me, though perhaps the weather only seemed extremely oppressive so due to the state I was in. I lay on my bed day and night. Periodically, Andrew would get me up, lead me to our dining table, put some food into my mouth and I would swallow it but bring it back up instantly. Andrew felt strongly that even the action of retching could start something going. I went through this process until I could no longer retch, and the food refused to go down. He would then put me back to bed and start again after I had rested. All through that summer I lay in bed or on our living room floor.

It was school holidays. David was 13 and, as usual, had lots of friends who came to our place. They would step over me as they went about their usual activities, such as playing sports outside. Some nights they camped across the road in the bush, arriving at our place for breakfast. I was surrounded by life and action as I went through the wilderness of my state, fighting for my life. Richard was 16, Natasha 10. It must have been horrendous for them to see me like this. I was helpless and appeared to be quietly slipping away from life. Yet, the five of us made it.

"Please let me go, the pain is beyond me," I said to Andrew many times then, "I just want to keep still, close my eyes and wake up in God's world."

Andrew refused to even consider that option for a moment. He would pick me up and walk me to the table to try just one more time to feed me. It took more than three years before I was pain free.

I had travelled a long way from my time of joy and Sister Kate's children, but it was that experience that changed a lot for me. Life had lost its carefree side. There were still a lot of challenges once I regained my strength, though. I was invited to take classes at a learning centre, basically in fitness and nutrition, and I enjoyed that immensely. I started again in my own home with exercise to music and, little by little, my life came back together. I wanted to make great changes, lead a simpler life, get away from the rat race, but this was not easy. However, I did make several subtle changes.

I don't really know where to go from here. A lot of what happened in the next decade involved a lot of people, including my growing children. In all that I experienced since marrying Andrew, I had full support from him. He never stood in my way, no matter what I tackled. He gave me the freedom to choose and encouraged me. He supported and admired me for who I was and what I was trying to do: to live as was right for me, to reach out to others.

Mind you, he had the same freedom to follow his paths in life and very often I tried to help him follow his dreams, particularly with his dentistry: to teach people how to care for their teeth and not have them break down at all. Teeth that are not subject to decay will last a lifetime provided you know how to care for them. This had been Andrew's dream and, in trying to realise it, he has been up against the whole profession, which was opposing him every inch of the way as he tried to bring about change. I not only supported his dream but helped him to try and realise it.

Throughout my entire adult life, being part of a church has played a big part in it. It gave me direction, nourished and comforted me, led me on a search for God and a closer relationship to Him. It has produced more questions than answers, but has, at all times, reaffirmed my belief. The reality for me of God and Jesus provided great comfort at all times. My search had its roots in atheism in Russia, and in the destruction and devastation of war and all that followed after 1945. Nothing made much sense, except that out of it all I concluded that where there is so much evil, there had to be an opposite, which was love.

It took a lot of living for me to arrive at some answers. When they came, it was all so ridiculously simple, because we are not puppets but creatures of choice, and it is the choices humans make that lead to either joy or its opposite. My belief is that God does not send us pain, war and destruction. Humans do that to each other when they lose touch with God.

Epilogue

After recalling so much immense sadness, particularly the death of my little brother, I was not prepared for reliving something that happened so many decades ago. This and so many other bad incidents made their way to the foreground of my mind instantly. It amazed me how all the living I had done since was suddenly pushed to the side. It must still be in the depth of my experiences and soul.

On completing my writing, I felt drained, but then focused quickly on the joyful parts of my life and sought comfort in them.

My adopted country, Australia, gave me a new start, a second chance in life that I made the best possible use of. Yes, it was built on the foundation of my childhood, but the choice to build a meaningful life or let myself be consumed by childhood trauma was mine. I chose the first option.

I had a good adult life. I faced many challenges and completed some to a high degree, others not so well. However, I tried to the best of my ability, which was important to me: I doubt even God expects more from us. Having loved and married an Australian made it a lot easier to adjust to my new world. I must also add that I never felt a victim. My mother's simple philosophy of good being more powerful than evil stood me in good stead then, and continues to do so now.

Another way of looking at my traumatic past is that it was all part of the formation of my character. How could I regret it? And yet, there is one regret, or should I call it sadness, that remains, and that is losing my father at the age of five in such a cruel way. At the same time, his sacrifice had become a beacon of light in the darkest corners of my life. It gave me strength and assurance that evil can be disarmed by the choices we make. We have a God-given choice, and are equipped with the ability to choose between good and wicked.

I also believe that we are all linked to each other by existing on this planet at the same time. All our actions have an effect on someone else. As with a pebble thrown into a pond sending ripples all the way to the water's shores, so our actions affect others. To focus on love and compassion, we must do as Jesus said: "Do unto others as you would others to do unto you". Simple, but true.

At times I wonder how I would measure up if I was tested in the same way my father was. He was only 29 when he had to choose between becoming a tool of evil or fall victim to it. He had no doubt or indecision, he just knew he could not become a tool of such evil. He was well aware of the consequences of his decision, yet he still made and stood by it. He knew he could not go against his conscience.

Sixty years on, my sister Irma still cannot talk about that night. She is still afraid of the consequences. My mother died without returning to that night. I found writing of it all very helpful, but was not prepared to experience that writing would take me to that time and relive it all over and yet, I am glad that I did.

Facing the horrors of that night, acknowledging it, has made me feel more comfortable. I know now what I am dealing with and have no ghosts or fear of the unknown.

I cannot imagine what it takes to do what Peter Gertzen did. He also knew of the persecution that lay ahead for his wife and children. At the end of my life, I often think of this handsome stranger whom I knew for only such a short time.

He passed such an eminent test and paid with his life.

I have written my story of a time before the fall of Russian communism. And now, since the fall, a lot of business-people from all over the world have made their way to Russia to cash in on the inexperience of the Russian people in terms of free trade. It is only free for the ones who get there first. They have the skills in business that the most Russians do not possess. The Russian system has kept its people ignorant and they are used to being exploited. I find this very tragic.

Will the Russian people ever have a 'fair go', or will someone always be there to exploit them?

That is my question!

Acknowledgements

As a teenager, I was one of the many 'waifs and strays' Lina Graebner took under her wing and showered with her seemingly endless love and attention. For a station kid in a strange city and at boarding school, the house in Lesmurdie was an oasis of care, excitement and attention.

I knew something of her story and of Russian history, but until reading Lina's diaries I never really appreciated or understood the traumas that Lina, her mother and sisters experienced in their escape from communism. These four incredible women endured and suffered so much, and it was a story that needed to be told. I am in awe of their resilience and bravery.

During my adulthood, I lost regular contact with Lina, but knew that she was writing her story, and also knew also that the process of writing was important for her own wellbeing. In later life she had many further health problems requiring extensive surgery, and life continued to unfairly send her many emotional and physical challenges. Her faith, wisdom, and endless love of her fellow human beings helped her through these challenges, as they had during her traumatic childhood.

I am ever grateful to Andrew Graebner, as well as Richard, David and Natasha for entrusting Lina's diaries to me. I am also grateful to Lina's still-living sister, Irma, who filled in many gaps as well as providing some minor corrections.

Thank you also to Rosanne Van den Broeck, a close friend of Lina's, who typed up the original diaries.

Lina, unfortunately, passed away as I was preparing this book, and so she did not live to see her memories published. It has been an enormous privilege being trusted to prepare Lina's story for publication.

Jenny Kroonstuiver

About Jenny Kroonstuiver

Jenny Kroonstuiver is a family friend. Born in the 1950s, she spent her childhood living on pastoral stations firstly in western Queensland and then on the Nullarbor Plain in Western Australia. During her high school years she spent a considerable amount of time with the Graebner family. Jenny trained as a teacher and spent several years teaching in country areas of the Northern Territory and Queensland, before returning to Kalgoorlie in the 1980s. After a short-lived marriage, she raised her four children alone, continuing to work in the broader education sector. From 2004, she took up a role managing the national training system for the Australian meat industry, a role she held until her retirement in 2020. Since then, she has been researching family history and this is her fifth book.

Also by Jenny Kroonstuiver:

Glimpses of Jean: The story of Jean Zuvela-Doda
Winton: The Swann Family Story
They came to Glengallan: A family history
Before the West